MONASTIC WISDOM SERIES: NUMBER TWELVE

Francis Kline, ocso

Four Ways of Holiness for the Universal Church

Drawn from the Monastic Tradition

D0877290

MONASTIC WISDOM SERIES

Patrick Hart, ocso, General Editor

Advisory Board

Michael Casey, ocso   Terrence Kardong, osb
Lawrence S. Cunningham   Kathleen Norris
Bonnie Thurston   Miriam Pollard, ocso

MONASTIC WISDOM SERIES: NUMBER TWELVE

Four Ways of Holiness for the Universal Church

Drawn from the Monastic Tradition

Francis Kline, ocso

Foreword by
Ladislas Orsy, sj

Afterword by
Michael Downey

CISTERCIAN PUBLICATIONS
Kalamazoo, Michigan

Cistercian Publications

Editorial Offices
The Institute of Cistercian Studies
Western Michigan University
Kalamazoo, Michigan 49008-5415
cistpub@wmich.edu

*The work of Cistercian Publications is made possible in part by support from
Western Michigan University to The Institute of Cistercian Studies.*

Library of Congress Cataloging-in-Publication Data

Kline, Francis, 1948–2006.
    Four ways of holiness for the universal church : drawn from the
monastic tradition / Francis Kline ; foreword by Ladislas Orsy ;
afterword by Michael Downey.
       p.   cm. — (Monastic wisdom series ; no. 12)
      ISBN 978-0-87907-012-0
       1. Holiness.   2. Monastic and religious life.   I. Title. II. Series.

BT767.K58 2007
234'.8—dc22

                                   2007023043

Christ d'Aric

The crucifix on the cover now hangs in the monastic refectory at Mepkin Abbey. It is the gift of Charles and Madeleine Combier, and their family. Its provenance is the village of Aric in the Ardêche (Central France). In the early 1900s Philippe Hêritier, the father of Mme. Combier, obtained the cross from the priest of the village church in exchange for a St. Sulpice-type crucifix, i.e., something more suitable to the time. It had been put aside because it was "scaring the children"! The label affixed to the verso of the cross states: "Christ du Xllième, provenant probablement du Prieuré d'Aric qui dépendait de la Chaise-Dieu." The Priory of Aric, a dependency of the Benedictine abbey of Chaise-Dieu, at one time set on the hill above the town, which built up after the priory's foundation some time in the 11th or 12th century. The priory dwindled while the town continued to grow. The crucifix was most probably part of the furnishings that left the priory at the time of the French Revolution and found a home in the parish church. From its somewhat naive character the piece looks to be folkloric, a creation of the devotion of a craftsperson of the region. Therein lies its beauty and devotional power. While there is no way to date it precisely, the position of the feet suggests a post-13th-century date.

When the Combier family came for the blessing of the Christ d'Aric in the monastic refectory, with much joy and emotion they said that they felt that at last it was where it should be, back in a monastic home. To them the monks of Mepkin are eternally grateful.

"Consider your own call, brothers and sisters;
not many of you were
wise by human standards,
not many were powerful,
not many were of noble birth.
But God chose what is foolish in the world to shame the wise;
God chose what is weak in the world to shame the strong;
God chose what is low and despised in the world,
things that are not,
to reduce to nothing things that are,
so that no one might boast in the presence of God.
He is the source of your life in Christ Jesus,
who became for us wisdom from God,
and righteousness and sanctification and redemption,
in order that, as it is written,
'Let the one who boasts,
boast in the Lord' (1 Cor 1:26-31)."

For My Brothers at Mepkin Abbey

TABLE OF CONTENTS

FOREWORD

by Ladislas Orsy, SJ

Dom Francis Kline, Abbot of Mepkin, once told me how he became a Cistercian monk. He was well on the way to being a concert organist when his progress was disturbed by a gently pressing call "to give himself to God." (Had the prayerful music of Bach played a part in it?) At any rate, he reached a point when he "knew" that his vocation was in a religious community but he was not sure as to where to go. He decided to visit several with one criterion in his mind: he wanted to find a place that was transparent in truth; that is, where the members lived up to what they preached—with no compromise. His probe ended at the Abbey of Our Lady of Gethsemani; there he found what he wanted. He asked to be admitted, he was accepted, and thus he became a Cistercian monk.

In this event of his youth the two qualities that marked his later life were already present: an all-pervading desire for God and a resolute rejection of any compromise.

He composed this book shortly before he died; by his own word, he had little difficulty writing it. He just poured out what was on his mind and heart. As the illness, which eventually took his life, was encroaching on him, he gave us documentation as to whom he was and what occupied his spirit. On virtually every page, he confesses that God is holding him irrevocably and that to surrender to this divine grip is an endless struggle for him. He experienced extreme sufferings in body and soul: "God crashed him" (his own words). But at the end Francis "knew" that his weakness had to be manifest, so that the strength of God may be revealed in him. At the end, Francis understood it all.

He gave an objective title to his work: *Four Ways of Holiness for the Universal Church Drawn from Monastic Tradition.* Yet, behind the expositions and exhortations, there is a subjective story. He could have called it *Confessions*—following Augustine's example. He is never a mere observer or cool theorizer; even when he writes about the great problems of the human race, or the need for renewal in the church, or the daily rounds of monastic life, he is revealing his own internal world. In a hardly veiled manner he gives us his own life story: how God pursued him through times good or bad, and how his eyes became more and more open to this divine presence, and how his will blended into God's desire.

Dom Francis lived in a monastery and he loved solitude but he never built an enclosure in his heart. He had an acute sensitivity for the joys and sorrows of the human family and for the glories and failures of the Christian churches. Whatever happened outside reverberated in his mind and his heart. As an abbot, he cared for the environment around the monastery and beyond; he worked discreetly and forcefully for the unity of the Christian churches; he helped as he could for the renewal of the local Catholic church.

For years Dom Francis pondered the question: **What can the monastic tradition give to the church—and through the church to the world?** Monastic tradition for him was not an ancient monument to be revered and preserved, but the source of light and strength that can give a renewed vision and fresh strength to the Christian churches and indeed the whole human family.

He found the answer: **holiness** is the gift that monks can give to the church and to the world. This holiness consists in the "transformation of the monk into Christ" through the power of the Spirit, so that the world could see Christ and hear his saving message afresh.

He was well versed in old and new monastic literature, and he was obviously inspired by it. But on these pages he is not propounding any abstract theory industriously gathered from books. No, he is not a "systematic theologian." He is speaking about God from the abundance of his heart. He is familiar with the Word of God, he is "at home" with the Rule of Benedict, and—principally—he is obviously a faithful listener to the Spirit of God.

He is not saying or implying that there is no flourishing holiness outside monasteries; such absurdity is far from his mind.

But he affirms that in the house of God, that is, in the church, there are many mansions, and for the well-being of the whole body some mansions must be dedicated to an intense encounter with the Spirit—for the benefit of all the others. A monastery is a place *par excellence* for such an encounter; the monks are "predisposed" for it by their separation from the world, in their radical silence, and through the control of the passions.

The book divides into four parts: *Conversion, Suffering, Desire,* and *Unity*. They do not, however, form a linear sequence; rather, each conveys the core message—in its own distinctive way. They overlap and intermingle; from the beginning to the end each is concerned with holiness. *Conversion* offers guidance for the rugged path to it; *Suffering* reports on Francis's own progress towards it; *Desire* tells of the love that is the driving force of the search for it; and *Unity* describes how holiness can make the church and the world "whole" as God always intended them to be.

Let these chapters unfold in greater detail.

Conversion is a long process toward "the reconstruction of the human person in the Risen Christ." Such a reconstruction, of course, can be only a divine work. But we can dispose ourselves by trying "to peel back accumulated layers of false identity" so that we may discover our own "hardness and coarseness of heart." If we make progress, we become aware of "the contrast between the paucity of human merit and the abundance of divine mystery." To be converted then means to be lifted up into the contemplation of that mystery. Initially much depends on our effort; at the end it is an effortless gift of grace.

Suffering is *Confessions* in a strict sense; Francis composed it in a personal and existential mode. There is no pretense in it. It is a piece of stark honesty: it does not cover up hurts; it does not call pain a delight. If the sufferer is blessed, he does not feel a celestial hand. The chapter recalls Jacob's struggle with God throughout a long night. And a night it was for the Abbot—more than one. He was stricken by an illness, insidious and devious: at times letting earthly hope rise—only to dispel it at a later time. When the best medical treatments could not halt the spreading of the disease and all seemed lost, Francis showed a new strength: he asked to be discharged from the hospital; he decided to return

Four Ways of Holiness for the Universal Church

to Mepkin and wait there for another call—from a place distant and close where "there is neither crying nor pain any more" (cf. Rev. 21:4).

Desire is rich in overlays. It could bear the title "In praise of contemplative life." Seemingly, it is an objective exposition of the "monk's path to God," of a monk driven by a stirring desire. But the alert reader will soon sense that this manner of speaking is just a literary device for Father Francis to say more about his thirst for the Absolute and his attempts to pierce the veil of the Mystery. As he progresses, he clarifies the meaning of desire. It is nothing less than love of God poured into a human heart—as St. Paul describes it in the hymn on charity in his first letter to the Corinthians (cf. 1 Cor. 13). When a monk receives the gift of this love in his heart, "the Spirit accepts his offering of sacrifice, scoops up the precious contents of his life, and distributes them to those elsewhere in the church who may need them. The offering of the monk is complete." Here, Dom Francis the writer is perfecting his thought: the gift of monastic tradition is not "holiness" in some abstract way, but holy monks, as concrete as they can be in their daily existence; they are earthly creatures sustained by grace.

Unity rounds off and completes the understanding of holiness because no holiness can exist without "wholeness"—without unity of minds and hearts among the disciples. The church is always in need of such "regeneration," so is the whole human family. The ultimate source of this gift is not in any created being but in God's "ecstatic generosity." Through his grace, we can play our part in this "divine emanation" when we "love God and our neighbor with the same kind of free abandon." Such love knows no limits; it includes all who were made to the image of God. This wholeness is already present—really—if only in some communities—in the celebration of the Eucharist. The kingdom of God is with us.

Dom Francis's writing is not for hasty reading. His insights were born in the silence of the monastery and matured in the turmoil of hospitals. He learned to comprehend "what is the breadth and length and height and depth" (Eph. 3:18). His thinking cannot be absorbed in a few hours: his exposition has its own measured rhythm—like chant in a monastery. To savor his sentences, the reader must adjust to their timings.

He was most himself when he was presiding over the celebration of the Eucharist in the monastic church at Mepkin, surrounded by the monks and the guests. His homilies flowed effortlessly from the readings: he let the Word of God unfold. He spoke to those present, but again and again he directed their sight well beyond the walls of the church and he made his listeners aware of the hidden thirst of all God's children for living waters and their hunger for the bread of eternal life. Better, he made them aware of God's desire to nourish them—God's children.

While he was anchored firmly in the wealth of the Christian tradition, he lived intensely in contemporary history. He was perspicacious in diagnosing the ills of our society as well as the shortcomings of the visible church—fragmented by divisions. But he did not indulge in complaining: he was in constant search for remedies. Even his casual conversations showed how much the needs of the church, local and universal, and how the miseries of the human family were on his mind.

Dom Francis—no matter how much he was fascinated by the heavenly—never ceased to be a down-to-earth, practical person. If nothing else, the funds he collected for the improvement of the physical plant of the abbey prove it. He lived with all his senses in this earthly creation. He could enjoy a festivity with the friends of the monastery around. He could delight to no end in the gentle beauty of the meadows and woods by the Cooper River. He could pray intensely by playing the organ. And he could carry on to some length a spirited conversation over a bottle of good wine.

His theology is a collection of insights into the Mystery that at some point overwhelmed him. He was captured by God's immensity and could not escape God's "ecstatic generosity"—no matter how frail was his own humanity. He tells his story in a fragmented prose that at times verges on poetry (after all, he was an artist) and in eloquent passages that often turn into meditations in slow motion.

We can return now to the question that he pondered in good health and bad: **What can the monastic tradition give to the church—and through the church to the world?**

Here is his answer, distilled from the four chapters and confirmed by many of his talks and conversations:

God has raised up monasteries to have sources of regeneration for the Christian communities. In a monastery, the beginnings of the church are replayed and reenacted—in God's own ineffable manner. As the apostles Andrew, Simon, and Philip and the others heard a voice, "Follow me," so did the monks, each of them. As the apostles followed the Messiah—at times with little faith and with great misconceptions about the kingdom of heaven—so did the monks. Poor and weak as the monks may be, the Spirit is at work in them: he gives them an understanding of the words of eternal life; he surrounds them with signs and wonders; he grants them enough resilience to persevere. But, since the apostles had to drink the bitter chalice of suffering, the monks cannot escape it either. On the day of the Crucifixion, the proud group that was ready to die with their Master fell apart; they dispersed dispirited in the desolate city. The monks must go through a similar experience: although they are in the monastery, at some point in their lifelong journey they must enter a night of hopelessness where they become disturbed and disoriented; they feel "crashed" and powerless; they can only cry for help out of the depth. But, as it happened in Jerusalem, it happens in the monastery too: the dawn breaks the darkness of the night, and the one who was dead and put in the tomb reveals himself: he is the Risen One. As Christ once restored the fear-stricken community of the apostles, he now reaches to his monks, heals them, lifts them up, gathers them, gives them one heart and one mind, and anoints them with his Spirit to be witnesses of his resurrection, witnesses of "the ecstatic generosity of God."

Under God's providence, the mysterious events of "conversion, suffering, desire, and unity" which once took place in lands of Judah and Galilee are taking place—ought to take place—in humble monasteries spread out all over the face of the earth. God has provided a source of perpetual renewal for his church. Monks are—ought to be—by God's design—contemporary witnesses to the power of Christ's resurrection. This is what monastic tradition —or the Spirit's ineffable action in monasteries—can give to the church: a community of Christians, in the most authentic sense of the word.

That is how Dom Francis Kline answers his own question. Over more than three years, the physicians did all they could to restore the health of the Abbot—with poor results. They reached the limits of their science and could offer little hope. But by then he "learned a new knowledge not found in books," and he "left the hospital [in New York] with a new heart and a mind refreshingly liberated."

He set his face towards the Abbey on the grounds of the ancient Mepkin Plantation, where the simple beauty of the church, the organ filled with prayer, the library rich in monastic literature, the garden displaying native plants, the majestic trees and the gentle meadows around the river, the slaves' cemetery recently restored and honored, and above all, his monastic community, were all awaiting his return. Resolutely, he went home, never to leave Mepkin again. There, when his hour came, his Maker found him.

The body of the third Abbot of Mepkin is resting under a simple cross by the monastic church; the daily rhythm of chants echoes over it. Cistercians do not put any praise on their tombstones, but if they ever did, a fitting inscription for the third Abbot of Mepkin would be: "Dom Francis, God's organist."

Ladislas Orsy, sj
Georgetown University
Washington, DC

(For the sake of simplicity, words and expressions in this Foreword taken from Dom Francis's text are in quotation marks but without further reference: the reader will find them with some frequency.)

ACKNOWLEDGMENTS

The abundant quotes from the Scriptures are taken from the New Revised Standard Version. The quotes from the Psalter, however, are taken from the Grail Translation (1963) which is the version sung in the choir at Mepkin Abbey. In the case of the Rule of St. Benedict, I have used the "RB 1980" edition. Inclusive language has been the goal throughout the book. Yet, in references to the Persons of the Blessed Trinity, masculine pronouns are used. In the case of the Father and the Son, the choice is obvious. For the Holy Spirit, I have followed the usage in the NRSV. The use of the compound subject "monks and nuns" has been adopted universally in preference to the awkward word, "monastics." In cases where an extended spiritual episode is described, I have chosen the single subject "monk" to lighten the prose. I mean the word to be generic.

The opening chapter first appeared in a somewhat modified version as an essay in *A Monastic Vision for the 21ˢᵗ Century*, edited by Patrick Hart, ocso, published by Cistercian Publications in their Monastic Wisdom Series.

Francis Kline, ocso
Mepkin Abbey
Moncks Corner, South Carolina

INTRODUCTION

Monasticism is seen in some quarters today as a panacea for what ails our culture. Many have unlocked the treasures of the monastic tradition and brought out meditation-like practices, concepts and attitudes that have helped the people of our time cope with the myriad brutal aspects of present-day existence. My concern in this book, however, is how to set in order the treasure house itself, as it relates to the church. Many of the valuable items inside have become devalued or have gone out of taste in today's changing ecclesial climate. I speak of authentic separation from the world, radical silence and effective control of the appetites. We have been the beneficiaries of magnificent scholarship which has made us aware of the challenge of updating our monastic thinking. Perhaps we need to introduce some new treasure into our house to make better sense of the old, not just for ourselves, but for the sake of the whole church.

In particular, we need to address what is spiritually distinctive, or theologically cogent, in the monastic church which removes itself to a "deserted" place in order to pray, when all of the rest of the church is concerned about the youth, vocations to ministry and religious life, re-evangelization, etc. We are no longer talked about or admired, or even known in many parishes, except by caricature and/or hearsay. The church, while caring for us, does not promote us in a way in which it once did, when priests and religious brothers and sisters talked fervently about the contemplative monks and nuns. The universal call to holiness, beautifully enunciated in the document *Lumen Gentium* of Vatican II, puts religious all the way back at chapter six, and insists, quite rightly, that they enjoy ". . . a special gift of grace in the life of the Church and may contribute, each in his own way, to the saving mission of the Church (*Lumen Gentium*: c. 6, n. 43). Yet, the Council

1

document, and other further legislative documents in its wake, seem intent on placing religious, without bothering to speak directly or particularly to contemplative monasteries, in a broad category of those professing the evangelical counsels of poverty, chastity and obedience. These are not the ancient monastic vows of obedience, stability and conversion of life. Nor do these documents explain what is unique about the contemplative, monastic tradition, source of so much of the prayer spirituality of the church. Nor do they posit a clear place for this tradition in the new structure of the church seen as the Pilgrim People of God.

The task of redefining our place in the church must come from us and from our lived experience before it can pass into ecclesiastical documents and legislation. The Council, by its call for the renewal of religious life, invited us to do this work. Monks and nuns have responded generously by reflecting on their lives in the light of the monastic scholarship of the recent past. Our new OCSO Constitutions (1990) represent a thoroughgoing elaboration of our Cistercian tradition as we are called to live it in our time.[1] Yet, what is still lacking in such a successful document is a clear indication of our place in the church in the light of the universal call to holiness. Our tradition, as part of its renewal and thrust into the future, needs to reflect on and articulate its own ecclesiology.

The foundations for our place in the church are going to have to be (re?)discovered from our own lived experience, which may then feed academic and theological reflection. In this book, our own practice of *Lectio Divina*, that is, prayer with the Scriptures, will be the *locus* for new ways of holiness, which then flow into a proposed new ecclesiology. But while we are making our way there, we see immediately that any monastic holiness is really a universal holiness that is valid everywhere because it comes from the Gospel. Monks and nuns may use unusual ways to get there, such as withdrawal from the world, celibacy, etc. Yet, the only possible difference between a monastic holiness and a universal holiness is that we take the same holiness to the very heart of the

---

[1] The latest edition of the "Constitutions and Statutes and Other Legislative Documents of the Monks and Nuns of the Cistercian Order of the Strict Observance" is found at www. ocso.org.

Scriptures, which is where every holiness is ordered and where every holiness finds its source. From the heart of the Scriptures, therefore, the monastic church offers to the universal church an eternally and refreshingly new insight into the Christian mystery. Monks and nuns do this in response to a direct gift from the Holy Spirit. Thus the unity of the holiness of the church will be revealed in all its manifestations, high and low, far and wide, as well as the real, true and eternally valid place of the monastic tradition or its equivalent in the church.

This book is elaborated from a thorough reading of the Scriptures in *Lectio Divina*. It makes no pretense at theological sophistication. It comes from one monk's prayer experience with the Word of God. The insights offered here are garnered from long monastic practice but intensified in the last several months by serious illness which has taken me away from my community at Mepkin Abbey and thrust me frequently into the hospital. I have had ample time to test my monastic way on any number of challenges thrown at me by my new situation. Very often alone with only the Scriptures, I found a voice of conviction about the monastic church and the universal church. Faced with end-of-life issues, I found the courage to say what has long been locked up in my heart, except for the occasional homily or conference to the monastic community. Methodical, academic exposition is my desire, but it is not God's will for me. Instead, I speak what I hear in *Lectio Divina*, and I reflect and draw conclusions from what I have read in the monastic tradition, as well as scriptural exegesis and dogmatic theological studies. Everything I read helps me to understand the Scriptures. I argue from them and apply them to the monastic texts I read and experience in the monastery. What I have discovered is that the monastic texts often reveal truths, even dogmatic truths, when they base themselves on the Scriptures. But they make such revelations when they are lived, not as brittle texts for conversation or edification but when they are trusted to bespeak the experience of living persons who wrote down what they had learned about God from their own lives. Thus, the Rule of St. Benedict becomes life-giving when it passes on an actual tradition of experience of the Scriptures. Because it is such a monastic distillation of the Gospel teaching, the Rule can guide me and affirm my own experience with God. Without this textual mentoring, I would not know how to interpret or use the gifts that the Spirit gives to me. I speak especially of the more contemplative insights around the Christocentric economy of salvation as the most salient way to read the Scriptures, and the relation of the missions of the Son and the Spirit, not as dry dogmatic truths but as we live them and feel them, particularly as they change the way in which we are invited to pray. These insights are hinted at in the monastic texts I read. The Spirit draws them out and helps us make the connection between experience and Revelation. Theology, dogma, spirituality, and praxis all converge in the human person when the Spirit finds a willing heart in which to raise up Christ. The Spirit makes us one with Christ and moves us beyond prayer to Christ, to prayer with him and in him, as he stands making intercession for all our brothers and sisters before the Father.

The promise of *Lectio Divina*, to pour out on the faithful reader a personal insight and conviction about some aspect of Revelation, finds tentative fulfillment in these pages. The Spirit provides unique insights into the mystery of God, insights which are valid in the Tradition and not new to it, but which take on a particular luster because they have been loved so much in the human heart. When the insights find voice in a book, even though they will never add up to academic theology, still, they may render the writer that exalted title of old: "Theologian," one who has had an experience of God.

All of us have had spiritual experiences. What is written here comes from a particular challenge of separation from my monastic community and the longing for it, and the subsequent time and even urgency to put voice into writing. The second essay, on "Suffering," autobiographical in nature, explains this separation. All four essays give birth to the conviction of the lasting validity and inherent value of the tradition which has given me such abundant life.

As a beginning, I propose four ways of holiness: 1) conversion of life as the preeminent model for the Pilgrim People of God; 2) suffering, or the cross of Christ, as the inevitable but faith-based yoke of the Lord, which he makes to be easy and light through love of him; 3) the desire for God which overtakes all other desires and stands thirsting before God who is desire; 4) the unity of all things in God, which appears as an emerging reality in the hearts of those who are willing to follow the Gospel teaching to its literal end. Each of these ways is particularly addressed by the monastic tradition. Each way depends on the other three and, altogether, continues the reflection and introductory work of the Council when it called the whole People of God to holiness.

The first task in each essay is to highlight the concept as a way of holiness for the universal church. Then, the monastic tradition is brought to bear on the concept in order to illuminate it and advance it. If the concept is universally valid, yet only adequately or fully explained by the monastic tradition, then we can see a connection between what the church lives, in its pastoral, everyday activity, and what the monasteries "do" to further the work of the church in ways that only the contemplative monks and nuns can effect. The monasteries appear to be more than a spiritual appendage to the work of the church. Instead, they emerge as the sentinels of the way to the church's fulfillment of its mission of evangelization. We are then in a position to suggest the ever-ancient and ever-new place of the monastic church in the universal church.

Francis Kline, ocso
New York City
Feast of the Conversion of St. Paul, Jan. 25, 2006
Solemnity of the Founders of Citeaux, Jan. 26, 2006

ESSAY I

Conversion

"Lord, make me know your ways.
Lord, teach me your paths." (Ps. 24[25]:4ab)

Introduction. We work out our salvation in fear and trembling (Phil. 2:20). In other words, we work out our baptismal grace in a continuous way. Baptism starts a dynamic process in the individual that ends or, one should say, is consummated in death. All through one's life, daily we hear the call of the Lord to follow him further up and into his own journey to the Father in the Spirit.

Great and sudden conversions play a part in this process of the baptismal grace, but they are no substitute for it. They must be seen as turning points, pivotal events, perhaps, that lead us to more subtle conversions as we continue to work out our salvation until the end. Dramatic conversions, tumultuous changes, even ideological ones, where we want to turn our backs on former positions we have held so dear, still must be seen in function of one grace, one offered salvation, guided by God's merciful hand.

Newman's quote rings as a clarion call for this idea of conversion: "Growth is the only evidence of life."[1] We work out our salvation in time, in salvation history, in which as individuals we seem to play such a small and anonymous part. Yet the long line of individuals and God's way with them is what constitutes

---

[1] John Henry Newman, *Apologia pro Vita Sua* (Longmans, Green and Co., London, 1924) p. 5.

salvation history. God wants a relationship with me personally. He is not accessed by old pieties in new circumstances. He had already explained the danger of putting fidelity to him, a living, breathing presence in our lives, into old practices where he may have been in the past but is no longer (see Mt. 9:16-17). We cannot access him by cultural freezing, as if rigidity and mere conformism to the past can substitute for the inspiration of his live-giving Spirit here and now. Of course, like scribes, we bring forth from the church's treasure house things both new and old, but we do this from the storeroom of the myriad traditions of the church with the guidance of the Holy Spirit (see Mt. 13:52). Blessed by God, the old things we bring out or retain, carefully and with discretion, reinforce and illumine the one Tradition of the church to be discerned all through salvation history even in so many and varied guises and appearances.

Ideas, practices, self-identities, however, are not easily abandoned, nor should they be. Yet, the Christian life, and its baptismal grace unique to each life, calls us to follow on the road after the Savior and enjoy his intimate company where the kingdom of God breaks out like so many wildflowers along the roadside in spring. We travel light, in the sense that our ideas of ourselves and of God are apt to be challenged and cleansed of their delusions rather frequently. And a readiness to follow the law of love and selflessness, especially when it comes to dealing with abusive and abrasive people (= enemies) is demanded. Jesus put it succinctly: "Repent (or change), and believe in the good news" (Mk. 1:15). This conversion will be called out of us, not just once, but repeatedly, until it finds the fertile soil deep within our hearts. Conversion is not a happening so much as a way of life.

The concept of salvation history can help us here. Some may think that it is the narrative history of God's holy people, Israel, and fulfilled in the church, the People of God. But the far truer understanding of the concept is the way of God with his People. The form of narrative history gives way, in the eyes of faith, to a description, no matter how poor or inadequate in our human language, of God's thoughts, directions, and saving power in his ultimate care for his people. The Scriptures always take God's perspective, never Israel's, so that the sacred writer can lament Israel's stubbornness and stiff-necked attitude, yet never defend Israel's behavior over against God. As salvation history moves out of the Old Covenant and into the Christ event, the church is seen as the definitive move of God toward us in Christ Jesus under the ever-present aegis of the Holy Spirit. Here, all wrong-doing, sin, and guilt melt away under the overwhelming and purifying light of God's mercy on us in the Paschal Mystery of Jesus. Narratives of infidelity, punishment and lamentation over the loss of God's presence in the Old Testament are superceded by God's continuing presence in the New Testament when Jesus goes to his Father and sends the Spirit among us.

Our personal salvation history follows the course of our baptismal grace as it directs us through our development of learning right from wrong and suffering the consequences of our wrongdoing. From there, we move to the acceptance, sometimes soon, sometimes not, of Christ as a living, intimate presence in our lives and our vigilant and repentant response to him throughout our lives. The baptismal grace can be seen most clearly when it leads us to reinterpret constantly our sinful, and/or confused or abused lives in the light of God's mercy and forgiveness. Even and especially the misfortunes we have lived through may become revelatory of God's constant providential care in this temporal and woeful world. The baptismal grace always leads to a deeper understanding of God in our lives, and this by means of our constant turning to him in moments of grace. Instead of considering our lives as righteous or not before God, we can turn and consider his ways with us, and celebrate him in his goodness. In our personal lives we are invited to make the move from the Law and the Prophets, which speak of Christ, to the putting on of Christ in Baptism and its way of constant, ongoing incorporation into him.

Some Characteristics. "I have not gone after things too great nor marvels beyond me" (Ps. 130[131]:1cd). The Christian people have discerned certain guideposts or road maps in the process of living out our baptismal grace that are valid for all times. We begin to notice a certain pliancy toward our neighbor. The imperiousness of a strong ego-intellect, so often a characteristic of youth, gives way to a tolerance and even deference to the opinions and judgments of others. Far from relinquishing our own ideas, we learn from others to modify our positions wisely for the sake of a richer attitude and a more universal stance.

There are no shortcuts through or detours around the process of the baptismal grace. No matter what our station in the church, no matter how many gifts of the Spirit we may seem to enjoy, we cannot depend on these to arrive at an automatic sanctity. They provide us with a way and a means to holiness. The grace bestowed, however, presupposes a "disponibilité" to receive it at depth so that within our vocation or state of life one may continually turn toward God in whatever journey the Spirit suggests in an ever-deeper purification of one's life.

Continual conversion implies also a growing capacity to "understand" and accept, according to the will of God, all the events of life, especially those which go contrary to personal ambitions, desires or perceived destinies. Glibly we pray in the Lord's Prayer, "Thy will be done." But only the grace of holiness can begin to lead us through the temptation of personal delusion and self glory, past the great trials of life, to a full acceptance of God's will for us throughout the drama of our lives.

Our personal history is the place where the baptismal grace is located. Chronic or terminal illness, the death of loved ones, opportunities almost grasped, then lost, may sour us and leave us discouraged. God uses these means not as punishments but as opportunities for us to rethink our program in the light of God's Word, and in the light of the passing nature of this world. If our misfortunes were punishments, how do we account for reversals in the lives of those we believe to be good? Or should we ascribe our calamities to God, who wills to punish us? How would our relationship with God proceed beyond fear of a malevolent and implacable authority? The answer to these questions lies in the passing away of all temporal things, in the angst, pain and revulsion toward it, which the Scriptures tell us is the product of sin and moral corruption which we see and experience in the world. This is not God's doing, but ours, insofar as we share in the collective human sin. Only with time and repeated conversions of our point of view, can we own our part in this tragedy.

The Monastic Response. "And he (Peter) took him (a lame man) by the right hand and raised him up; and immediately his feet and ankles were made strong. Jumping up, he stood and began to walk, and he entered the temple with them, walking and

leaping and praising God" (Acts 3:7-8). Having briefly examined the process of conversion in anyone's life, we must now consider the monastic response to the same holiness. The Cistercian contemplative tradition identifies stages in the life of conversion. With the basic monastic ascesis in place, that is, separation from the world, silence, control of the appetites, etc., we begin to peel back accumulated layers of a false identity, a "persona," which we show to the world, but which hides from ourselves the unpleasant aspects of who we really are. And there stands revealed, especially to ourselves, a vulnerable, often frightened person prone to sin. In the strength of God's grace, that fresh-skinned person is more free to love the Gospel, to follow along the road after the Master, and to be more pliant to the promptings of the Holy Spirit. According to St. Bernard, in his first published treatise, "The Steps of Humility and Pride," the immediate effect of a serious dose of self-knowledge is a compassion and understanding of our neighbors in all their foibles and imperfections.[2] Self-knowledge levels off our own false high self-esteem to the point where we see ourselves equal to our neighbor. St. Paul would recommend seeing ourselves lower than our neighbor and counting others better than ourselves. This Pauline doctrine bases itself not on a poor self-image produced by a wounded personality but on the touch of God, who, as he approaches the human person, burns away pride and ambition. The purified one automatically sees others in a noble light, perhaps even as God sees them, as his precious children. Freed from the unnecessary baggage of false perceptions and attitudes about ourselves, our neighbors and the world, we know a joy and a freedom not to be compared with any of our former possessions. We become like the healed cripple who walks and leaps and praises God.

Obviously, one undergoes many such conversions before arriving at a humility in the continual presence of God. Cleansed from sin and vice, and loving, as if naturally, Christ and his Body, the church, the penitent approaches the source of all Truth, God himself, by the power of the Holy Spirit.

---

[2] *Sancti Bernardi Opera* (Roma: Editiones Cistercienses, 1963) vol. III, *Tractatus et Opuscula*, "De Gradibus Humilitaties et Superbiae," n. 6, pp. 20–21. In English.

With God in sight at all times, one faces the reversals and misfortunes of life with new eyes. Nothing can separate us from the love of God in Jesus Christ, neither cancers, nor death, nor hurricanes, nor earthquakes, nor betrayals in the community. In fact, these "bad" things can become good things, or, if not good, then blessings, if they lead us to plumb further the depths of God's love. This new vision defines more clearly what it is to be a contingent being in the palm of God's hand, and it qualifies life in this temporal world by letting us see that it is no longer an end in itself, but the gateway, and the only one at that, to God and his heavenly kingdom.

As a conclusion to this presentation of the concept of conversion, both along its general lines and with monastic precision, we may say that the reconstruction of the human person in the Risen Christ constitutes the very essence of the Christian life when viewed in its ultimate and eschatological perspective. The constant call of the Savior's voice, through the faithful celebration of the sacraments and adherence to the Gospel teaching, awakens a faith in the human person which goes deep enough into the will to rehabilitate it and allow it to follow the Savior through every suffering, every trial, even unto death. This conversion is to begin to live eternal life even in the here and now of this world. It invites the human person to become "spiritual," in the Pauline sense of the word, to put on Christ, to be mature in him, to leave behind childish ways of the flesh, that is, an understanding of Christ according to a human point of view (see 2 Cor. 5:16), and to "press on toward the goal for the prize of the heavenly call of God in Christ Jesus" (Phil. 3:14).

Given Jesus' call to conversion, growth in the spiritual life, and how the monastic tradition views both, we must ask the question: Which way from here? Is conversion better to be seen as a means to the kingdom of God, along which we discover other ways, such as continual prayer, acceptance of suffering, control of the appetites? Or does it describe something more fundamental about the human person before God? Is it perhaps a structure of being according to which we are all shaped as God approaches us and we approach God in the Paschal Mystery of Jesus? And if this is so, shall we not find evidence for it in the Scriptures themselves, and especially Jesus' teaching and experience in the Gospels? And if we shall adopt it, shall it not appear in the church, and in the church's self-understanding? It remains for us to examine the Gospels and to trace the lines of conversion in the lives of those who interacted with Jesus, heard his preaching, and "vowed" to be with him to the end. As we do so, we shall discover, as if never before, where the particular emphasis of conversion in the life of monks and nuns came from and why monastic life can be understood fully only in the light of this particular holiness. From here, we can also see how conversion to Christ, with monasticism close by, lies at the heart of the church.

Models of Conversion. "Sin speaks to the sinner in the depths of his heart" (Ps. 35[36]:2). The encounter between Jesus and the penitent woman in the Gospel of Luke (Lk. 7:37-50) serves as a model for repentance in the Christian church. It shines as a grand and sudden conversion such as we see in the life of St. Paul and many others in the history of the church. But though it is sudden, it was perhaps prepared for an extended time. In such great hearted souls, where there may have been a strong and long-standing refusal to a call from God, we see the anatomy of grace. God eventually topples their refusal, and once freed from their blindness, their love for God proves stronger than their former iron resistance. What seems to be a dramatic and immediate turnaround could have hidden a protracted and bitter struggle between the person and God.

In her great act of repentance, the sinful woman behaves nobly and courageously by boldly coming to Jesus and disregarding the religious laws and social customs surrounding that encounter. Her love, based on God's forgiveness, overcame all obstacles and won for her the object of her spiritual desire. Henceforward, in the Christian church, the heroic conversion of the great sinner become the great saint serves as a paradigm for repentance and a reminder that with God, all things are possible.

An even more probing example, and one that introduces us into the very Paschal Mystery of Jesus, is the behavior of the apostles in the Synoptic Gospels, but especially in the Gospel of Mark.

In the first written Gospel, the apostles exhibit a slowness to understand Jesus' mission and person. Time and again, Jesus finds them incredulous, self-absorbed, or cowardly. In the end, they abandon him. The other Synoptic accounts, that of Matthew and Luke, soften the failure of the apostles, and, in the Gospel of John, Jesus himself excuses them. But in the Gospel of Mark, nothing softens the harsh exposure of the apostles' weak faith in and betrayal of Jesus. Indeed, in all of the Gospels, nothing except the death and resurrection of Jesus alters the pattern of the apostles' behavior.

Signs and wonders do not soften the hearts of the apostles to believe that Jesus is God. Having multiplied the loaves and fishes for the five thousand, Jesus dismissed the crowds and bade his disciples to get into a boat and go ahead of him to the other side. An adverse wind had them straining at the oars. He came to them walking on the sea. They took him to be an apparition and cried out in terror. He spoke to them to comfort them and got into the boat with them and the wind ceased. The Gospel text tells us at this point that "they were utterly astounded, for they did not understand about the loaves, but their hearts were hardened" (Mk. 6:51-52).

Jesus' power over the elements, a sure sign of his divinity, terrifies the apostles but leaves them perplexed. They recognize the power just demonstrated before them, but their hearts are too thick with materialism and tradition for them to confess Jesus as Lord. They cannot yet believe that this teacher in front of them, who looks like them and befriends them as a fellow human being, is also the God of heaven and earth. After all, the Scriptures are full of the majesty and power that surround God, either in his theophanies at Sinai, for example, or in the sanctity and ritual that surrounds his presence in the Temple at Jerusalem. The God of heavenly glory they would recognize; the humble teacher in front of them belongs to this world. He is one of them, even though he performs signs. The Holy Spirit cannot yet break through their hardness and coarseness of heart. Their tradition blinds their eyes to the truth of what they are seeing. They do not yet understand that God's omnipotence allows him to come among us, to hide his divinity, and, from time to time, to break forth in glory by exercising his authority. Nor do they allow that God in all his majesty, surrounded by celestial powers "with cloud and darkness as his raiment" (Ps. 96[97]:2a), would ever be interested in them and in their petty concerns on the lake of Galilee.

The kingdom of heaven as the intimate presence and action of God in the very person of the Teacher in the here and now seems to be Jesus' point as he tries to convince the apostles after the second multiplication of the loaves. Knowing that they had only one loaf of bread with them in the boat, that is, not enough for a meal, Jesus cautions them against "the yeast of the Pharisees and the yeast of Herod." But they confuse his image of the yeast with concern for their supper. Jesus then becomes explicit. "Why are you talking about having no bread? Do you still not perceive and understand? Are your hearts hardened? Do you have eyes, and fail to see? Do you have ears, and fail to hear? And do you not remember? When I broke the five loaves for the five thousand, how many baskets full of broken pieces did you collect? . . . Do you not yet understand?" (Mk. 8:14-21).

The apostles do not yet understand, presumably , because they still are permeated with the yeast of the Pharisees, that is, a trust in religious observances and ritual instead of trust in God. The yeast of Herod, too, that is, a materialism which blocks religious faith, keeps them from believing in the kingdom of heaven present and acting in Jesus. In his company, they need not worry about their lack of bread. They need attend only to one thing, his presence among them. Everything else, including their daily bread, will be seen to by God. The trust in God's intimate and providential care in one's daily life is what is offered by Jesus in his signs and in his presence. Yet, the apostles keep lapsing back into a religious safety net, the yeast of the Pharisees, where God is distant and accessed only by ritual deeds. In this vacuum, a materialism based on what one can get for oneself, the yeast of Herod, substitutes for God's saving presence in the physical and temporal world.

The lessons imparted to the "wicked and perverse generation" of the apostles continue when he comes upon them in the embarrassing act of their argument about who was the greater. He calls them aside and teaches them the unforgettable doctrine: "Whoever wants to be first must be the last of all and the servant of all" (Mk. 9:35). To demonstrate his teaching, Jesus calls to himself a little child whom he takes up in his arms as the least and the most vulnerable. To be last must mean to go to the last, to be with them and minister to them. Likewise, any who are ill, possessed or thought to be unacceptable are the objects of the ministry of Christ's disciples. For as he did, so must we. While others may argue about who is the greater, or may spend their time and energy looking to be acceptable and appointable by the powers of the age, the Christian minister must be seeking fervently the last place where Christ is to be found—with his friends, the children, the poor and the outcast.

The most confounding failure of the apostles in the Gospel of Mark occurs when, having just celebrated the Passover meal, they go out with Jesus to the Mount of Olives and abandon him there as he is arrested by the crowd sent by the chief priests, the scribes and the elders. This desertion comes after and on top of their protests that they would never abandon him. Peter himself asserts that though everyone else may desert him, he will not. Jesus replies with the terrible prediction that Peter will deny him three times before the cock crows twice on that very night (see Mk. 14:30-31).

This enervating and deplorable action by the apostles is expressed in the starkest terms by the evangelist to highlight the extreme contrast between the paucity of human merit and the abundance of divine mystery. That we are dealing with the will of God, even in the failure of the apostles, becomes evident when Jesus quotes the prophet Zechariah, "I will strike the shepherd and the sheep will be scattered" (Mk. 14:27 [Zech. 13:7]). God wills that divine power should be made most manifest in human weakness, and not in human strength, which, when puffed up in the human heart over against God, is an abomination to him.

This prediction of the apostles' failure by the prophet lies in direct continuity with God's way with his people. He leads the Israelites on a circuitous route so as to allow the Egyptians to catch up to them. Thus, when God acts at the Red Sea, the people could never conclude that it was their speed, their strength, or their cleverness that saved them from the Egyptians, but God alone (see Ex. 13:17-22). At the failure and the death of Saul and the crushing defeat of the Israelites by the Philistines, it is the bravery of David, an insignificant subordinate but inspired by the Holy Spirit, that turns the tide of victory for the Israelites against their enemies. Not Saul's stature, nor his anointing as king, could make his heart right with God so that he could lead Israel successfully. Only the coming of the Holy Spirit upon

David could change the military situation of Israel (2 Sam. 5:17-22). God's power is made obvious and glorious in human weakness and failure. The behavior of the apostles must be seen in the light of the stark contrast between our broken power and God's ultimate mercy.

The evangelist dramatizes the failure of the apostles by underscoring in sublime detail the denials of Jesus by Peter, the appointed head of their circle. Peter it was who led the protest against Jesus' assertion that they would all become "deserters." Peter said, "Even though all become deserters, I will not." And when Jesus retorts that on that very night before the cock crows twice Peter will have denied him three times, Peter vehemently insists that "Even though I must die with you, I will not deny you. And all the apostles said the same thing" (Mk. 14:27-31).

The scene is set for the evangelist's careful and effective intertwining of the narrative of Jesus' prayer at Gethsemane, his arrest and "trial" by the high priest and the chief priests, with Peter's denial of Jesus, the last and lowest of the long list of sad behaviors of Jesus' intimate circle. When a servant girl of the high priest spots Peter in the courtyard warming himself as Jesus' trial proceeds, she stares at him and says, "You also were with Jesus, the man from Nazareth." Peter denied it and went on to deny again that he was one of Jesus' followers, until a third time "He began to curse, and he swore an oath, 'I do not know this man you are talking about'" (Mk. 14:71).

Peter curses and swears not just against Jesus but against himself and all the apostles whose leader he is. In the anatomy of his relationship with Jesus, i.e., his vehement and impetuous declaration of love for Jesus (". . . I will never deny you" [Mk. 14:31]), contrasted with this coarse cursing and swearing that he did not even know him, we see to the bottom of the human heart, not just of Peter, not only of the apostles, but of everyone. We see our utter inability to do what we want to do, because of a previous commitment made to Satan, shrouded in the mists of time and dismissed by the mind as untrue or unfair. Yet, our world, broken by war, violence, and greed bespeaks the bitter truth. The mess we see is our doing. It is Satan's miserable victory over us, stretching back from the Garden until now. Yet his victory is not final. And this is where we need to keep reading in the Passion

Narratives to see what happens to the apostles once Jesus rises from the dead.

As the apostles scatter in fear, Jesus tells them that he will rise from the dead and go before them into Galilee (Mk. 16:7). His saving victory over sin and death will reconstruct their broken loyalty and their intimate circle and absolutely nothing else will. The striking of the Shepherd and his resurrection alone will reunite the scattered sheep, so that it may be made clear that no human virtue or strength remained loyal to Christ. Only God's power and mercy constitute the new community of the apostles around his risen body.

Conversion at the Heart of the Scriptures. "I will tell of your name to my brethren and praise you where they are assembled" (Ps. 21[22]:23). What we see in the Synoptic tradition and the Acts, but especially highlighted in the Gospel of Mark, is a model of repentance as the response to God's mercy in the Christ event. We see individuals fall and come to repentance, such as Peter, but we see them living out their repentance in a community who holds them in God's forgiveness. The early church's experience of human weakness in the face of persecution and memory of the failure of the apostles, guaranteed that the Good News of Jesus Christ would be preached only around the saving power of his resurrection. The Christian community would be based not on human merit but on absolute faith in the resurrection in a continual move toward greater and deeper repentance.

The apostles were gathered in prayer "with certain women, including Mary, the mother of Jesus, as well as his brothers" (Acts 1:14). What was their thought as they prayed in that space between the Ascension and Pentecost? Surely, they reflected on the miracle that the risen Jesus had reconstituted them as his circle. He had appeared to them through forty days, interrupting their attempts to return to a normal life, that is, a life without him. But he would not let them alone. And now, they were gathered at his bidding, waiting to be clothed with power from on high. Before the event of Pentecost, or, perhaps, because of it, their conviction about the risen Christ was made firm. Yet, part of that foundation had to be an eternal memory of their weakness. After all, they had abandoned him, and had tasted the nothingness of their own power. "Not to us, Lord, not to us, but to your name give the glory" (Ps. 113[115:1]:9).

One cannot help but notice the juxtaposition of Mary and the gathering of the apostles. A broken community, reconstituted by the power of Christ, is prayed for by one who never abandoned the grace of the angel but bore her mysterious Son and saw him through his awful fate—all by the power of the Holy Spirit, the same Spirit who was about to come upon the whole gathering. What she had learned about openness to God and the concomitant humility that goes with it ("He looked on the lowliness of his handmaid" [Lk. 1:48]), she now prays may be the apostles' joy as well. As she had given birth to Christ and presented him to the world at the meeting of Simeon and Anna in the Temple (see Lk. 2:25-38), so now the apostles would give birth to Christ in their hearts in a new configuration of their own persons. Open to his Spirit, they would present him to the world in all of its languages.

The Monastic Connection. **"I want to know Christ and the power of his resurrection and the sharing of his sufferings by becoming like him in his death, if somehow I may attain the resurrection from the dead" (Phil. 3:10-11).** The early monks and nuns, separated from this event of prayer in the Acts by several hundred years, nevertheless intuited that they were in direct imitation of the apostolic circle.[3] Not that they constituted the church. Not that their way of life was the only way to be a Christian. But, rather, in the conviction that what the Spirit was calling them to do by renunciation was in direct communion with the apostles' experience of the risen Christ, that is, the passage from considering Christ from a human point of view to a life permeated by his Spirit.

What is the content of the monastic imitation of the apostles at prayer with Mary, the women and his (Christ's) brothers? It is

---

[3] See John Cassian, *The Institutes*, trans. Boniface Ramsey, OP, Ancient Christian Writers, n. 58 (The Newman Press, New York, Mahwah, 2000), II, V, 1–3, pp. 39–41; *The Conferences*, trans. Boniface Ramsey, OP, Ancient Christian Writers, n. 57 (Paulist Press, Mahwah, 1997), XII, II, 5, pp. 436–437; XVI, VI, 4, p. 561; XVIII, VI, 1, p. 637.

none other than the passage from considering Christ from a human point of view to that of something else. Their point of view included themselves, and what he could do for them in their false idea of an earthly kingdom replete with power and privilege. Remember James and John asking the Teacher to grant them to sit at his right and his left in his (earthly?) glory? (Mk. 10:35-40). All of this died in the ashes of their failure at the Garden of Gethsemane. A new consideration of Christ was born in them after his resurrection. Its seed in them was a never-to-be-forgotten knowledge of their weakness. Indeed, the coming outpouring of the Holy Spirit upon them would reinforce it and enrich their preaching with it.

When the monastic tradition applies the apostle's experience of the Paschal Mystery, it does so in learning steps. Whereas the cataclysmic event of Jesus' suffering, death and resurrection was stamped forever on their minds and hearts, nevertheless, they learned from his intermittent appearances and the corroborating testimony of others to fashion fully in their beings the conviction of his saving power and merciful forgiveness. The monks and nuns, in imitation of the fifty days in the Lucan story of waiting for the Spirit (see Acts 1:12-14), adopted a similar mode of building. Step by step, and grace by grace, they learned to admit the saving word, a two-edged sword into their flesh so that it could work its purifying task (see Heb. 4:12). For the monks and nuns, the apostles' fifty days might be fifty years but lived in the same enthusiasm and urgency. For with the Spirit, there is no wasting of time nor vagueness of purpose. We see, therefore, a lifetime spent in the formation of the Risen Christ in the heart of a monk. This is the monk's own experience of suffering and dying with Christ so as to be raised with him in the full power of the Holy Spirit. Only the Spirit knows, and only the Spirit can direct those actions and experiences which lead a person through the great trial in imitation of the Lord Jesus. One passes from interpreting one's life more and more according to a Christ perspective as conversion occurs, to turning the corner in a definitive move by the Holy Spirit in one's life. Then, one considers Christ no longer from a human point of view. Rather, we can say with St. Paul, "forgetting what lies behind, and straining forward to what lies ahead, I press on toward the goal for the prize of the heavenly call of God in Christ Jesus" (Phil. 3:13-14).

Steps of humility, stages of conversion, levels of self-knowledge all conspire as so many graces to lead the Spirit to confer on the monk the crowning grace of passage to life in Christ Jesus.

The Monastic Church. **"Remember Jesus Christ, raised from the dead, a descendant of David" (2 Tim. 2:8).** The monastic church lives in the hope that each of its members will make this passage to live in Christ Jesus. Not all the members are granted it, not all are ultimately called to it. Not all answer when the summons is given, "for many are called, but few are chosen" (Mt. 22:14). Nevertheless, at the center of the monastic church, because of the gift of the Spirit which calls that ecclesia together, lies the memory of sin and repentance, that is, the desire and zeal to return to God and to keep turning toward him in the countless ways he asks us to follow. The memory begins with Jesus himself who stands before the throne as the Lamb once slain, or with the marks of slaughter still on him (Rev. 5:6). From that eternal memory of what he suffered for us, and what he achieved for us by his suffering and death, there flows another memory that wants to be joined to that of Jesus. The memory of his suffering illumines and activates the memory of sin and repentance in our own lives, so that, as we are drawn closer to him in his heavenly glory, our repentance and our continuing conversion grow brighter and warmer. The paradox lies in the growing focus of our memory of shame and guilt, even as we are drawn to him who saves us from it. Like one magnet to another we race along this journey, now not out of our own volition or energy, though that is active, but by a spiritual attraction to the Truth, overwhelming in its purpose and passion.

This is what makes the monastery the place of holy challenge that it is. Not because of the holiness of the monks who live there, not because the ground is made more sacred by the footsteps of their holy persons. For many of them may not be very holy. But because of the hope that lies in the heart of the community. In that hope, the action of the Holy Spirit who causes gifts of conversion, self-knowledge, humility, and so many more to flow back and forth until, and, if only, a single person lights up with the memory of the wounds of Christ in his heart and the consequent stance of repentance. This hope is what gives the monastery the élan and the spiritual peace it enjoys in the minds and experiences of visitors. With no means to explain what they sense, they nevertheless intuit that God is active here. After all, it is God alone who is holy. We but share in his holiness.

The monastic ecclesia holds up this hope of bringing people to the memory of Christ as if it were a single ray of light, warming and illuminating the whole church from within. As St. Benedict was given the vision of the whole world caught up in a single ray of light, so the monastic church, governed by his Rule, holds aloft the grace of the Holy Spirit for the whole church. Every other gift looks back to it as if to its source, for it is the source, insofar as it is the apostles' testimony to the Risen Lord. Every inspiration in the church breathes from this one maternal breath, this primordial grace which went to the heart of Peter at Jesus' three questions of love, or the heart of Paul, when knocked to the ground and blinded by the light of the risen Christ, was forever converted. So the monastic church is called apart from all other gifts and missions of the church, so that this light of Christ, which it guards, proclaims, and lives by, may guide the church on its way of return through all its manifold activities.

The Mystery of the Church. ". . . the kingdom of heaven is like a net that was thrown into the sea and caught fish of every kind; when it was full, they drew it ashore, sat down, and put the good into baskets but threw away the bad" (Mt. 13:47-49). The baptismal grace at the heart of believers calls them to many different positions in the church: to preach, to teach, to heal, to serve, to govern, to prophesy. Yet each of these missions is not an end in itself. Each is an avenue for the individuals to find the way of return in ever-deeper levels of their being. The Spirit will accomplish through them what it wills to do for the church. The Spirit will not fail, however, to offer the workers in the vineyard their own contemplative rest which is based on constant repentance and conversion. What is offered every baptized person is the call to follow after the Lord to the point of gratitude for the gift of life, self-knowledge, and repentance for sins and for the greatest sin, that of crucifying Christ. We all share in that greatest sin.

Yet, in the burdensome demands made by the missions of the church, the narrow way of living the gospel, as if in the intimate circle around our Lord, gets lost. The church has become endlessly complex in keeping with its mandate to go to all the world and preach the Gospel (see Mt. 28:19; Mk. 16:15; Lk. 24:27). We should never think that, in its missions, the church grows thin or attenuated. The same baptismal grace is as full of the seed of hope in the African infant as it is in the Cardinal Deacon in Rome or the monk in his cell. But each is called to repentance in so many different ways. What the church keeps forgetting inevitably because of its weakness is that holiness of life must follow the way of constant conversion, leading to a humble repentance.

The monastic ecclesia supports the wide net of the church by which many are called. It throbs with the missionary heart of the church in all its varied works. It commiserates with bishops as they carry the weight of pastoral anxiety. But with all of this outward activity, in which there is always the call to holiness emanating from the Baptismal grace, the monastic church keeps a light of memory on the way of return to the heavenly glory. It keeps revealing the structure of the church as both the wide net and the narrow way. It does so by taking the same holiness to which all are called, to the heart of the Scriptures from which the holiness was born. If there were no monastic church, the Spirit would have to raise one up. Only in such a way could the church be completely itself—a mystery in this world but not of it. Broad and welcoming in its preaching and pastoral zeal, yet not flinching from the deep truth about our sinfulness and the narrow way of return by repentance and obedience, the church can never be one or the other, but both as it proclaims a universal holiness wherever the Spirit is at work. The monastic church comes to the aid of the universal church by defining and keeping clear the narrow way of the Gospel all the way to glory.

The church was born into this human reality as Christ lay dying on the cross. The monastic church keeps alive the memory of that day and its glorious counterpart, the resurrection. At the foot of the cross and in the heart of the monastic church, the boundaries, rules and safety of this world's horizons begin to give way to a raw contingency, a radical dependence on God where the kingdom of heaven begins to break through on the moral light of this temporal world. Hidden to all but spiritual observers, the monastic church appears to make no sense, to be a collection of weaklings and losers who have thrown away their lives in a useless round of monotonous and unrewarding prayers. But to God, and to those who see with the eyes of God, it is where his light begins to shine on this finite darkness, where his strength shoulders human weakness, where human weakness is so known, tasted and accepted that his power can be admitted where human pride had previously shut it out.

The church makes no spiritual sense without this hidden gift of total surrender to Christ and constant conversion to him. It is the church's wedding garment which it only partially wears when it forgets the monastic way. The church is not its complete spiritual self without this total abandon to the love of God, this total joy of the freedom of the children of God, this total sacrifice which is held up as a single ray of light in the brilliance of which all the other gifts and ministries of the church shine.

Thankless, rootless, without a home here, unknown or derided, thought foolish and meaningless, the monks and nuns look out on the eastern horizon for Christ the Bridegroom of the church, in a world still too busy with itself, still too taken up with its own seriousness. The monks and nuns keep the church alert in vigilant waiting for the Savior. The monks hold aloft the light of the mystery of the church, still in this world but well on its way to full communion with the mysterious God. The light shines on, but in a fog where only the intently gazing can see it.

Mepkin Abbey
Exaltation of the Holy Cross, September 14, 2005

ESSAY II

Suffering

"Take away your scourge from me.
I am crushed by the blows of your hand." (Ps. 38[39]:11)

Introduction. In the other three essays in this book, I based myself on the practice of *Lectio Divina*, offered reflection on it, and narrated the experience that flows from it. But in this essay on the holiness of suffering, I turn directly to experience, because the immediate and suddenly revelatory nature of suffering requires instant reporting. Suffering disperses and fragments the energies of mind and heart into a thousand points of light and makes reflection on it a hazardous task. Then, I call upon *Lectio Divina* to gather around and reunite me into the reception of an illuminative message. A working definition of experience would be in order here. Experience of God is the urge we feel when God is breaking in on us at mind, heart, will or anywhere in our person, so that we, in the context of faith, are able to respond to him, immediately or eventually, in prayer and action.

As there are many famous and well-beloved books on suffering and end-of-life issues, I do not dare to compete with any of those. I only wish to penetrate as deeply as I can the experience of suffering I have undergone and continue to undergo, so as to clarify for myself what God is doing to me, in me, and for me. It may be of interest to others.

The adoption of an autobiographical mode in this essay is warranted, since suffering is as subjective as the human face. It is written all over it, there to be blended into the personality of the subject or to be rejected in chaos and bitterness and the reduction of the person. Suffering is a trial and a dangerous one at that.

One cannot write about suffering from a theoretical point of view. If one describes what one sees in another, that, too, is subjective. If one writes about one's own suffering, one ought to go deep into oneself guided by the Scriptures, in order to bring order to the chaos that suffering introduces. Memory, of course, plays the biggest role here for it molds and bends the facts according to the subject's experience. What may seem to be a not-so-bad situation to observers may, for the one putting up with it, be the feather that tips the scales. For suffering is cumulative, and the memory of it is selective and directional. It guides the mind toward the significant things in one's experience. From there reflection begins and insight is achieved, according to the Spirit of God who gives the grace of reflection. No one can enter another person's memory. So I have determined to take the plunge into the marsh of autobiography, in order to elucidate suffering, the second of these four holinesses. And it is from memory, with all its pitfalls, that I draw on for the material here.

The dates given here will be as accurate as files and consultations can get them. The places will be described without attempt at disguise. Those persons who are known to me outside of the medical staff are identified as who they really are, with no attempt to hide them. The names of persons who make up the hospital and medical staff under whose care I have been will be deleted, as will be those of my fellow patients, since I am still in the middle of this medical history and will continue to interact with them. Out of respect for them and all their colleagues at Memorial Sloan-Kettering Cancer Center (MSKCC) in New York, I will camouflage their identities. If they were to read this essay, however, they would recognize themselves. Otherwise, the essay would not be autobiographical nor the experience described be accurate. I have suffered with them and at their hands, all with a view of coming to some greater life, whether here or there. I have come to love them all, even if I have seen right to the limits of science, careful bureaucracy, and humanity's foibles which they represent. The juncture where human effort falls limp and the nothingness of faith must enter is what this essay is about.

The diagnosis. "Fear him; do not sin: ponder on your bed and be still, make justice your sacrifice and trust in the Lord" (Ps. 4:5-6). In May of 2002, the doctor for our Mepkin Monastery, outside Charleston, South Carolina, arrived for the yearly physicals for all the brothers of the community. After a good morning's work, he and his nurse were invited to a special lunch prepared in the small guest dining room off the monastic refectory. After I quizzed him on the state of the community's health, the doctor relaxed in his chair and assured me and the infirmarian that all the brothers were doing very well, considering the age of some and the proclivities of others. I was greatly relieved to hear his assessment, since one of my principal duties as Abbot is the care of the physical well-being of the brothers. After the usual pleasantries at the end of the meal, I accompanied him to his car outside the back door of the kitchen. He turned to me and said into my smiling face, "Everyone here is fine except you." Puzzled and not perturbed, since I felt just fine, I said to him, "What are you referring to?" He looked more serious, and somewhere between a clinical recital and deep concern, he told me that my spleen, a lymphatic organ, was greatly enlarged. It could mean several things, none of them pleasant. The most likely cause, he concluded, was that I had had hepatitis some time in the recent past which had left its mark on this organ. Considering where I have traveled as Abbot of Mepkin, to Africa and frequently to Latin America, the likelihood of contracting some kind of infection was high. But, to be sure, he wanted to order some tests, CT scans and the like, to see if, perhaps, something else more serious was afoot, which he would not pronounce upon until he had the test results. I noted the change in his otherwise pleasant demeanor, something I was to see over and over again in this journey, so I asked him to be more specific. "Cancer or perhaps HIV infection," he said bluntly and went on to emphasize that, until we had the test results, his leaning was toward the hepatitis effect.

We parted, he with his nurse to his car, and I to my office where I sat to ponder this message. I looked out the window toward the Cooper River, its broad expanse glistening in the high springtime sun, and what I saw were heavy clouds on the horizon, whether they were there or not. I felt something coming toward me that was not yet a threat, but whose slow and inevitable advance held mystery and adventure as well as deep foreboding. Being a monk, and steeped in the monastic tradition, I turned to what was at hand. We always respond to the concrete and immediate, which in our case is usually prayer, public or private. I exercised that discipline of the daily and the hourly schedule to help me take this threat inward to my inmost self, as day became night, and night became day, and there to ponder what this might mean. From there, and only from there, would I be able to formulate a response of concrete and actual behavior. First there was the local clinic where the tests were conducted. After coming out of the CT scan room, the nurse told me that I had to see my doctor right away, that there was something serious going on. She also had changed her countenance from cheery to apprehensive and almost abhorrent, as if she did not want to be around me. I left the clinic with a feeling of confusion. I did not feel ill, and I was able to keep an active schedule.

I traveled to Conception Abbey in Missouri to preach their retreat, and while there with those admirable monks and their splendid Abbot, Gregory Polan, I learned by telephone from the doctor that I had what he suspected was CLL, Chronic Lymphocytic Leukemia, an incurable disease, but one that could be treated and managed, and, in many cases, treated for a long time. I knew, of course, that my father had been diagnosed with this disease back in 1967. His being a mild case, he is still with us (2005). Back home at the monastery, after a biopsy of one of the swollen lymph nodes, the doctor confirmed his educated guess that CLL is what I had. He would call in a few days with the recommendation of an oncologist in Charleston whom I could visit. But first, an HIV test just to make sure that the CLL diagnosis was as accurate as could be.

Charleston is the biggest small town in the world. And Mepkin Abbey is a well-known institution throughout the Lowcountry, the various county districts along and in from southern coastal South Carolina. Not only from my visit to the local clinic in nearby Moncks Corner, but also from the node biopsy at Roper St. Francis Hospital in Charleston, the rumors that something was wrong with Abbot Kline were swirling. Nurses and doctors enjoy a huge network of communication, from their workplaces with enormous numbers of people coming and going, to their families and schools where their children attend, churches, etc. It wasn't long before the monastery received a trickling stream of calls asking what was wrong with the Abbot.

After the HIV test came back negative, and after first seeing my new oncologist at Roper Hospital in Charleston, we, that is, we within the monastic community and our PR director, Mary Jeffcoat, decided on two courses of action. First, that an announcement would be made at one of our two annual Piccolo Spoleto Festival events at the monastery. This was so that the cloak of secrecy and obfuscation that sometimes surrounds medical information would be opened and, indeed, torn apart. The second was that I would not be seeking any other help, in any other city or medical center, than in Charleston. I had no desire to escalate this still unknown quantity of an illness. Besides, Charleston is no mean city when it comes to medical care, and the monastery is on familiar terms with the medical community there.

After the oncologist told me that a regimen of chemotherapy would be in the offing very soon, our medical friends and consultants whipped into action by suggesting and procuring Chinese herbs, Japanese vitamins, and setting up appointments with acupuncture practitioners who claim to control nausea. Everything was ready for my first chemotherapy treatment. On the set day, I put a note on the bulletin board for the community, asking for their prayers and indicating that I would return sometime in the late afternoon or early evening.

When I arrived for the treatment, and after the usual taking of vital signs, the oncologist told me that I had bronchitis, along with a slight fever, and that he could not treat me in that condition. So he told me to take the antibiotics he would prescribe and to return in two weeks. This I did, and the same thing occurred. I could not get rid of the infection.

During all this time, I and the community were under siege from friends and well wishers begging us to consider alternatives to the present medical plan. Couldn't I go to the Mayo clinic, or the M.D. Anderson Center in Houston, or Duke University, or Sloan-Kettering for another opinion? There was even an offer from a wealthy monastery in Europe to go and seek the best medical assistance and that they would pay for it.

I found this first lesson in the psychological response to illness on the part of friends very confusing and unwanted. Illness is a very private thing. I felt as if folks were intruding into what was my very personal enclave. And, yet, I was to find that illness has its public attraction, that the curtain of privacy that surrounds the sorrow that is illness is pulled back by friends who want to show their love by participating in it somehow. Time and again

I have been told how helpless people feel when my subject comes up. They want to see me, tell me how they feel about my case, and what I should do about it. They want to share in illness's uncertainty and bring their own strength to bear on the patient. Though many sick people feel isolated by their disease, and even face death seemingly all alone, my experience is just the opposite. I have never been sick alone. The brothers of Mepkin, who of all have been the most respectful, the staff and friends of the monastery, as well as the volunteers and supporters of our outreach to the community, continue to make their presence and their care known and palpable. They want to make sure that I am still there with them and for them, primarily by phone calls, but also by cards and gifts and an admirable generosity that has helped to sustain our monastery through this difficult period. And, while, on occasion, the burden of friendship weighs heavily, the invitation to go out of myself is my surest sign that I am still in the land of the living.

Still, what to do about the suggestion of a second opinion plagued me and the community at the monastery, since it was coming through so loud and with stiff insistence. Determined to stand firm, but increasingly aware of the revolt at my back, I returned to the oncologist again for my first treatment. What he said surprised me: "Go to Sloan-Kettering in New York for a second opinion. I arrange this frequently for my patients. I have been in touch with them up there, and they will call you with an appointment. In the meantime, your first treatment is scheduled for two weeks hence." Whether the oncologist had been hearing of the growing chorus for a second opinion or not, I will never know. But I was relieved. I could satisfy the objecting chorus and still stay in Charleston for my treatment, and also travel to that storied cancer center in New York City that I had heard so much about, all by doctor's orders and not my own determination. Following the considered direction of the doctors, and not trying to doctor myself, but taking the appointments given me by the infirmarian and the doctors connected to the monastery, is an essential element in the monastic approach to modern medicine.

In a few days, a call came from Memorial Sloan-Kettering Cancer Center for the Treatment of Cancer and Allied Diseases, with my appointment in their referral service for leukemia for the second week in August. My first reaction was confusion. This appointment would come long after my treatments were to start in Charleston. Yet, all seemed to be in order, and the doctors surely knew the time sequence and what it would mean. So I was at peace. But peace was not to endure for long.

What I call the "Catholic connection," for lack of a better term, now came into play. David George, a former seminarian but also a nurse administrator at a local hospital and a close friend of the monastery, knew of the MSKCC referral date. He at once set in motion a series of phone calls that were to alter forever the direction of this medical journey. The Prioress of the Carmelite monastery in Elysberg, Pennsylvania, David's hometown, contacted a nurse, a close friend of this monastery, Kate Sullivan, who is also the nurse for the Chairman of Surgery at MSKCC. Given her position and prestige at the hospital (she has worked there for over thirty years and has been the nurse for the Chairman of Surgery for 21 years), she brought pressure to bear on the unofficial leader of the leukemia service, a man who has published more articles on leukemia and its research than practically anyone, and a gifted clinician. Everyone in the hospital seemed to know him and his reputation for fairness, tough-minded clinical care, and medical conservatism, that is, no treatments until they are absolutely necessary. Kate is a woman who gets things done and is not afraid to lean on the shoulders of the broadest and tallest. She begged the doctor to take my case and, incredibly, he agreed. Late in the afternoon of the same Friday that David began his phone calls, the eminent doctor's nurse called to tell me of my appointment with him on the following Tuesday.

Three of us went to New York—Fr. Stan, David George and myself—and were hosted by Msgr. Philip Franceschini, pastor of Our Lady of Pity Church on Staten Island and a close friend of the monastic community. He arranged for a car to take us into Manhattan and the four of us, joined by Kate, waited to see the doctor. He entered the examination room, after having seen my blood work and other tests, and sat himself comfortably in a chair, and began to talk in a manner that I would come to call his hallmark. A verbal technician, with a flair for tight images and an absolute command of statistics and stories of CLL patients, he regaled us for at least 20 minutes on how I didn't need treatment at this time; that, yes, indeed, I had cancer and a good deal of it; but that for the moment I was asymptomatic and, according to his book, needed only monitoring. He would gladly agree to be my doctor. I would need to see him periodically, as long as the cancer remained at this stage. Many people come to see him from all over the country, and he is used to accommodating schedules and awkward travel arrangements of those who come from afar. He even offered to call the oncologist in Charleston to explain the situation and to smooth over what I could see to be a potentially strained relationship with the Charleston doctor.

So began a honeymoon period with cancer. I traveled to New York perhaps four times a year and had several bumps in the road, as the doctor said, when my blood counts would rise and fall, causing some alarm. Yet, in the main, I, and all the brothers, felt that I was getting the best care, and that, for the time being, I was a fully functioning Abbot. The time of grace lasted until June of 2004.

After a routine exam at MSKCC almost two years later, the doctor noticed that my hemoglobin was dropping ever so slightly from the last time. "Something we should monitor carefully," he said. Iron medicine was prescribed and I was sent on my way back home with an appointment sooner than usual. From Charleston, I traveled by car to our monastery of the Holy Cross, Berryville, Virginia, at the Blue Ridge and the Shenandoah River, one of my favorite pieces of geography in the USA. On a shining summer's day at the end of June, outside on the lawn using the cell phone with the Blue Ridge at my side, I was talking to the doctor's nurse. I described not feeling well, tired, but more than that—no energy at my command, whereas up until the present, I could always call up reserves even when there were none. I just could. Now, I was needing more sleep, a mitigation I reluctantly gave in to, and one that challenged the monastic regime of ascetic control of one of the three primaries: sleep, food and sex. The reply over the phone was that fatigue could be caused by any number of factors, and I should not presume to label too quickly the cause of it. Discouraged, I went on with the retreat I was preaching to the monks there. Then, with the same car, I drove to my original monastic home, the Abbey of Gethsemani, where

I was to consult with the Abbot and play an organ recital on their magnificent new organ. Kentucky in late June is a splendid thing, and my spirits were not dampened even in the heavy rain which greeted my approach to the monastery. But the joy of being at my first home was dulled considerably by the growing fatigue, especially in the preparation and the presentation of a concert. It was perhaps my best effort as an organist, and I was glad for the opportunity of praying to God through music in a place that, through long struggles in monastic formation, had brought me to an integration with music, my monastic calling, and my union with Christ.

I rose for Vigils, the first service of the day at 3:15 a.m., but I did so as a soldier dragging himself to battle only at the command of the platoon leader. I tried to rest at intervals during these days of the visit, but I felt as though I never could achieve a satisfactory rest. The real proof was the drive home to Charleston, where I had to stop frequently to keep from falling asleep by resting at a fast-food place for coffee and an occasional ice cream.

Back at Mepkin, I sludged through my duties, did not consult with anyone, and hid my growing concern. Perhaps my age, 55, was now getting the best of me, after many years of cutting my time of sleep or rest down to the minimum. I believed in hard work and managed to keep, I thought, several balls in the air. First of all came my duties as monk and Abbot of the community. Out of this flowed an engagement with the local ecclesial and civic communities on whom Mepkin depends for its well-being. And deep from within me, there is the urge to make music, something I had disciplined for a long time, and whose flowering in my later monastic years had been one of the great joys of my spiritual life. It was my unique way of prayer, that is, of being taken over by the Lord. It made so many other things in my line-up of duties possible. Whenever I succumbed to the ascetic suggestion to forego music, I would always be drawn back to it, and always on a Feast of Our Lady.

Being an introvert, except when comfortable with intimates, I have always found the monastic role of Abbot to be a taxing one. Yes, I can speak in public and preach, and the success I have enjoyed has reassured me to keep at it, but the wrenching out of me of a good address or a public appearance takes its toll, and I quickly need the solitude of a monastic cell to come back to my inward home. In all this activity, I have developed the capacity to maintain my monastic prayer schedule, including meditation and *Lectio Divina*. This, I have always felt, has enabled me to do everything else.

That summer, in addition to my other duties, I was working on the piano part for the Franck A-Major Violin Sonata, a favorite piece, but one of the hardest in the chamber music repertoire. Being an organist, I rarely venture in public into the realm of the great romantic piano literature, yet here I was gearing up for this longed-for performance with a wonderful soloist in late September. It was hard going and is the best way I have of describing the cloud of fatigue that was lowering itself over me. While my fingers delighted in the daily new challenges of this piece, my ability to practice no more than an hour at a time, and even the effort it took to get to the practice room, told me this was going to be a long haul.

My fears were diminished somewhat when, in August, I traveled to Esmeraldas in Ecuador for the Regular Visitation of our daughter house there. The sisters, young, enthusiastic and melding their Caribe culture with the ancient monastic tradition, always provide me and any monk of our community who has gone there with a new enthusiasm for all things monastic. Not only did I rejoice in attending all the offices, but I even took up jogging again, which, as of late, I had been neglecting. Now I was trying to conclude that my fatigue may have been in my head, that my age was wearing me down, that 14 years of abbatial service, night and day, were finally catching up with me. I returned to Mepkin, determined to carry on and to drown the anxiety over my health in a renewed trust in the Lord.

At about this time, a terrible flu began making its way throughout the community. One after another passed on the symptoms: ache, stomach upset, slight fever, malaise, and the like. Because CLL compromises the immune system, I am always at the ready to go on antibiotics as soon as a cold begins that shoots up into a fever. I called the doctor in New York to report in. After beginning the regimen of antibiotics he prescribed, I felt comfortable and secure. But the cold, or whatever it was, never went away. Stomach problems continued to plague me. I couldn't rid myself of the cough, and every so often I would take my temperature and find a slight and mounting fever. After a few days of escalation, the fever would go away, and I would enjoy a space of normal living.

On September 10, 2004, a great grief lowered its massive burden on our community when our Brother Laurence was run over by his own tractor or backhoe. An enormous wheel crushed the entire lower part of his body. Airlifted to the Medical University Trauma Center in Charleston, Laurence began a hospital stay that was to last for months. The blow to the community was severe, and the toil of caring for him in the hospital, an hour's drive away, was strenuous. I visited him frequently, even though I knew it might not be safe. Yet, I thought, my job comes first until someone tells me differently. And taking care of Laurence and his needs and the medical consultations were not things I was willing to delegate. For I was still trying to keep my head above the water of this illness.

A visit to MSKCC later in September showed no appreciable growth of any cancer, neither in the bone marrow nor the blood. Only the hemoglobin still continued to drop slowly and the white cell count (and that of the neutrophils) was bottoming out. The doctor, suspecting an ulcer or polyp as the cause of the loss of blood, had already ordered a complete GI workup, which I had done in Charleston, and it turned up nothing. The doctor kept me on the oral iron medication, after a further infusion in the day hospital, and insisted that as soon as I arrived back from Europe I should see him.

Sick in Venice. "I am exhausted with my groaning; every night I drench my pillow with tears; I bedew my bed with weeping" (Ps. 6:7). The Order of the Cistercians of the Strict Observance has a regular offering of classes and discussions that initiate new superiors in their ministries. Every three years this course is offered in Rome in the three principal languages of our Order— Spanish, French and English. I was pressed into service for the English section and felt that I had to go, even with the serious case of Laurence on my hands. I played the Franck Sonata at the end of September, an evening of great beauty and joy but one in which I came several times to the absolute limit of my endurance, and left the next day for Rome. I remember dragging myself around to the classes, not caring anymore whether I appeared sick or not, and hoping for some end to this flu, or infection, or whatever I had. One evening in Rome, Dom Peter McCarthy and I visited Msgr. Franchescini and his pilgrimage group at their hotel, which was very near St. Peter's. We were all admiring the recently restored façade and its marvelous illumination. Febrile, I just kept staring at the dome, oblivious of the conversation around me. My eyes darted back and forth to the Pope's apartments across the square, which had been lighted but, one by one, had grown dark around the ailing John Paul II. I was feeling very ill with fevers and the sweats which accompanied them, yet, I remember this twilight time as a glimpse into the suffering of the church and my own anguish. The two somehow became one, enwrapped in the beauty of the dome and the warm halogen light on Travertine. I felt later that it was an entrance into another world, a world accessed through this one, and always in this one but also beyond it, and somehow deeper through and into it. My friends remarked afterward that I seemed lost in a reverie, sick and preoccupied and removed momentarily from them and, though physically right next to them, inaccessible. Abbot Peter and I traveled onto Venice for a few days before returning to the States. Once again, as in Rome, a physical weakness filmed my eyes as I studied the catechetical order of the mosaics in San Marco. Even as I celebrated their beauty and theological sagacity, I felt a dampening of my joy because this was now the past for me, and the future was the mists of God's calling, which could not be painted, or written, or performed, but only followed in blind faith.

By previous arrangement, I stopped in New York on my way home to see the doctor. After looking at me and my blood counts, he became suddenly perturbed. Everything had gotten a little worse. He told me that he was tired of chasing me down through the schedule I was keeping, that if I lived in the New York area he would be seeing me more frequently, and that he had to insist that I take time off and come to New York for a week of tests. I was obviously sick and he could not help me if I were not going to cooperate. As hard as this was to hear, for I thought I had been following instructions up until that time, I acceded to his request.

I carved out the last week in October to stay near the hospital in order to be tested with scans of all sorts and to undergo another GI workup. He was sure that the lowering hemoglobin count was due to the loss of blood coming from an ulcer or polyp or some other cause.

On the Thursday of that week, and after the tests, I dragged myself to the clinic at MSKCC, expecting to spend the day there and to catch an evening flight back to Charleston, where my parents were to meet me the next day for their annual visit to Mepkin. After the preliminary blood work, etc., the doctor came in and said, "You have a fever, you are very sick with an infection, and I want to hospitalize you today." I was horrified. I had made no plans. I had no more clean clothes. My schedule at Mepkin was full because of my absence in Europe. Brother Laurence's case was worsening. I had assumed that if I ever needed hospitalization, I would be in Charleston, where we had financial arrangements with the three major hospitals. I had been only an outpatient at MSKCC and had never countenanced the thought of being an inpatient there. I suppose I never really had anticipated this crisis. So I said to the doctor that there was no way I could go right away into the hospital. Oh, he said, it will only be for a week to ten days, so that we can get this infection under control. "I really can't let you out of here. You are too sick," was his reply.

The Patient Tower at MSKCC. "Who shall climb the mountain of the Lord? Who shall stand in his holy place" (Ps. 23[24]:3)? Entering Plato's cave might come nearer to the experience. The darkening tunnel into which I was wheeled (I was now in a wheelchair) can only be described as dull, humanless, worn down by science without poetry, and ugly. I waited in a holding room to be admitted into a room on the 12th floor, the leukemia floor of the hospital. Around the large, monochrome, beige-yellow room with fluorescent lights were arranged twenty or so wheelchairs with various types of humanity in them. In the center, as I was to find always in the center, was a large TV screen bawling out the latest gossip around the coming presidential election. Food? No, thank you. I had seen my neighbor picking her way through fried chicken and plastic-looking vegetables from a white box.

She was a vegan, and, after turning aside the chicken, she was chewing through the string beans. David George had come up from Charleston that day to be with me when I saw the doctor. He provided me with soda and peanuts. But he had to leave on the same flight on which I was scheduled to return to Charleston that night. I was alone, screening out the TV, sitting in the wheelchair with my few belongings in my lap, waiting to go to the 12th floor. Little did I know at the time that this hospital stay would remind me of the rarefied experience Thomas Mann describes in his famous book, *The Magic Mountain*, where love and philosophy, illness and surging emotional energy go hand in hand at an asylum atop a mountain in the Swiss Alps.

When I was wheeled up to the 12th floor, I came into a tunnel of black, for it was 10:30 p.m., passed a curtain, and found myself in a small partition of a room, with a hospital bed and some chairs. The ankle-length curtain revealed the feet of my neighbor (I hadn't planned on that) and the sound of a TV or movie. The nurses kept my part of the room in semidarkness. During the questionings necessary for a first admittance, I began to take in the surroundings and the situation. I had no privacy, I had no clothes, I had no routine and no schedule. And now I had this IV pole tethered to me, as a hairshirt or scourge might be "from the old days." The sense of dislocation and loss was extreme. From a monastic point of view, I was deprived of my observance. Yet, I was to discover quickly that the hospital has its own routine, to which I quickly adapted. Night passed into day and day into night, the first day. How to get meals, how to get cleaned, how to manage everything with this IV pole. How to, how to, how to . . .

During my first week in the hospital, it began to dawn on me that I was a monk no matter where I was, and this realization required several creative responses to new challenges to the monastic code. First, my neighbor. During the night, I began to be aware of not one person but two people in the curtained partition next to me. It took only a few days to learn that my neighbor was a young man whose family never left him for the night. Either an aunt, or father, or mother, or girlfriend stayed with him all the time. There was a reclining chair in his partition, as there was in mine, for such arrangements. You could see their feet, you could hear everything they said, except when they were talking occasionally in their Filipino dialect, and you could test their taste in television and films. They also cooked, or, rather, brought in improvised meals of the Asian sort that went through my nostrils and beckoned me into their sensuousness. They were a kind and devoted family, and the young man was a prince of a person. But I quickly learned that to make a request is to get two or three in return, and that no one wins the contest of controlling the environment. We shared the wide window looking east, but with a single shade, the chain being on his side. We shared the bathroom and had to negotiate the time of just about everything. We understood that extra visitors just had to be tolerated with increased talk of a more exuberant quality, as well as the TV, until well into the wee hours of the morning.

I made several conscious decisions. Keeping in mind the Rule of St. Benedict at chapter 36:

Let the sick on their part bear in mind that they are served out of honor for God, and let them not by their excessive demands distress their brothers who serve them, (RSB 36:4)

and remembering also the Sermon on the Mount:

You have heard that it was said, 'An eye for an eye and a tooth for a tooth.' But I say to you, Do not resist an evildoer. But if anyone strikes you on the right cheek, turn the other also; and if anyone wants to sue you and take your coat, give your cloak as well; and if anyone forces you to go one mile, go also the second mile. Give to everyone who begs from you, and do not refuse anyone who wants to borrow from you (Mt. 5:38-42).

I resolved to make no demands until it became absolutely necessary to obey the doctor's orders. I resolved to cede control of the environment to my neighbor, no matter who it was, no matter how demanding or callous. (The idea had not entered my head how systematic this torture would end up to be.) I resolved to turn the other cheek when, corrected by one nurse, I was, for having complied, upbraided by another and told to do something different. I came to realize that not even reading, or music, or any other distractions could blot out the inner voice that kept urging me to delve into the spiritual "space" I had been gifted with during this hospital stay. Along with the resolutions, the further ascetic practice of keeping still and quiet, sometimes by just staring out the window, developed into the experience of a gift to be savored and protected, rather than a discipline to be adopted.

My joys were the early morning light passing from darkness which I could see out of the window facing east. Even if the shade was lowered, you could still discern God's sun and its radiant face. Some patients could only see the three towering smoke stacks in Queens, or the distant subway trains, or the block apartments on Roosevelt Island. But I could see the stretch of enormous eastern sky with its dramatic sunrise overpowering every human building on the horizon. I could also view the tugboats on the East River as they moved in between the buildings on the riverbank. I could enjoy the food, such as it was, for it was always new and unexpected, even if horrid at times. I could appreciate, most especially, the neighbors, who were only too quick to make friends and to share "war stories" of their illnesses. I could bask in the tender care of the nurses, whose praises I will always sing, who never seemed to lose patience, whose young, lithe female bodies (for the most part) were a source of delight, and who could always be counted on for pleasant conversation.

The hospital regimen was strict but with a benign face that everyone took care to maintain. Yet, immediately below the surface, there lurked all the impatience, backbiting, and vengeance of the violent world which we all know. Monastic community living had trained my intellectual senses to spot these difficulties. I felt it was my call as a monk in the hospital to call out these demons when they emerged to engage me from under the skin of the admirable clinical culture of the hospital. Time and again, one could calm down another, by offering patience when they were expecting a fight. For always, beneath the surface of a raging passion, there was a human being trying to reach for the light, who, in the frustration of not reaching it, turned briefly into an armed soldier with a will for battle, to make right a slight, to honor falsely a battered heart, or out of poor judgment to return in kind the perceived evil in their face. The search for the true human face and occasionally the finding of it behind my false perceptions, whether brought on by cultural anomalies, behavioral quirks, or my own shyness and fear, became my greatest joy in the hospital.

It was a difficult regime that I carved out for myself. Yet, I felt energized in doing it, even if I failed and had to apologize to someone. But the ceding of the control of the environment and the tempering of a complaining tongue when, for the hundredth time, a new Heparin lock had to be stuck into my hands or arms, proved to be only the initial foray of the battle. The final assault on my fortress was to come.

"Like a Lamb Led to the Slaughter . . ." (Is. 53:7). During the course of this first hospital stay, the doctor prescribed the most powerful antibiotics known to medicine, and these were infused intravenously. As the weeks wore on and because of the medication, my veins, never large, became hard and rubbery. As a result, I could not sustain a Heparin lock, that is, a needle-like catheter in my arm or hand for intravenous medication for more than two days. The normal is four, and for a child it is sometimes seven. At the end of a brief life of a Heparin lock, my arm or hand would either swell large or throb with pain or both. The IV nurses, or phlebotomists, became wary of 1218A, my room, because of the difficulty in finding a good vein. From my perspective, some of them were good at finding veins, while others were not. Sometimes the nurse would ask me to find a vein or, at least, tell her/him where they should poke for a vein. I found this very confusing and awkward. I was asked frequently why I did not have a MediPort, a permanent opening to a vein somewhere in the chest that could be left closed when not used or opened easily when a blood draw or an IV line was required. I needed a blood draw every day and always after the rise of a fever (for the taking of blood cultures) and, as I said above, a new Heparin lock about every day and a half. The number of "sticks" in my arms has probably been in the hundreds since my hospitalizations began, because I have had one or two or three "sticks" every day for at least a hundred days in the hospital.

One day, I was wheeled out of the room to be given a MediPort, something ordered by the doctor on the floor, at the request of a number of the IV nurses. Leaving the elevator on a lower floor where the procedure was to be done, an escort interrupted me to say my own doctor was intervening and changing the order for the MediPort. His unalterable position was and is that MediPorts are too much a risk for infection in leukemia patients. As unreasonable as this sounded to everyone else concerned, I was to become convinced through personal experience that my tough-minded doctor had his reasons for this decision.

Yet, the number one difficulty during this first hospitalization was the growing sense of loss and separation from my community. After the first week turned into the second week and then the third, it became clear to me that I could not participate in or even attend the annual Benefactors' Concert at Mepkin around the date of November 14th, the founding date of the monastery and the anniversary of the dedication of the church. This was an important function in which we celebrate that most ancient and solemn of monastic feasts, the Dedication of the Church, and the blessing of the graves of our brothers who have gone before us in the sign of faith, and where we connect with our benefactors and friends. It is arguably the most important monastic function of the year, a feast peculiarly our own and dearly beloved by all the monks. My absence was unthinkable, yet here I was, helpless in this hospital room, with a growing realization that this infection, or whatever it was, was not to be rid of easily. I still had no image of myself as being that sick. There was certainly no threat of death, no tumor that could turn lethal, no disease in any organ that would require surgery. I began to feel out of place among others on the floor who had much worse conditions than I seemed to have. Yet, here I was in the hospital as a patient for (almost) the first time in my life, and I could not get out, nor did I have any idea when I would be released. All the doctor would say was that I had to be a week or more without a fever. The most I could achieve was three days. Every time it seemed that my condition was improving, I would strike another fever, sometimes as high as 103 degrees. At every fever, the doctor would say, "another ten days."

At the Benefactors' Concert that November, it was announced that I did not have a second cancer on top of the first, that I was hospitalized for a bacteriological infection that was difficult to bring under control, an infection brought on, no doubt, by my suppressed immune system (due to the CLL), and that I would return to Mepkin as soon as the antibiotics did their work.

In the meantime, a second important date was approaching fast and slipping out of my grasp. The diocesan congregation of The Sisters of Charity of Our Lady of Mercy in Charleston, one of the oldest congregations in the USA (1829), was having its 175th anniversary celebration at the end of November. I was certain that by that time I would be back home. But as the days of the Thanksgiving holiday rolled by and I was still spiking fevers, I knew that another monk would have to take my place for this most important function. I was beginning to feel like Job who said, ". . . the Lord gave, and the Lord has taken away; blessed be the name of the Lord" (Job 1:21b).

Was I slipping into some kind of permanent sickness? Was I never going to get out of this hospital? Would I never return to myself, as my body weakened and lost weight, as my muscles atrophied from the lack of exercise, the heavy medication, the fevers, and the lack of interest in food? In the mirror, I appeared as a cadaver, repulsive to myself. In the eyes of visitors, I could be animated enough but looked weary and sad and gray. The only human consolation I had was the occasional visitor and, above all, the nurse, Kate Sullivan, who visited me daily and usually twice daily, who brought me soup from a local deli for lunch, who did my laundry and occasionally brought in a splendid evening meal, as she did on Thanksgiving Day. Refusing to eat meat, in keeping with the Rule (c. 39:11), I was greatly reduced in what I could eat from the hospital menu. And Kate was religious minded enough to respect that and to help me make up for it by supplementing my diet wherever she could.

My spiritual consolation was the celebration of the Eucharist in the hospital room. When I was able, I celebrated Mass daily with other patients on the floor in my hospital room. But on Sundays, Msgr. Franceschini, whom I will honor all my life, would drive into Manhattan early in the morning, beat the traffic and celebrate Mass with me in the hospital room by 7:00 a.m. The beauties of the liturgical year rolled by, one by one: the last Sundays of Ordinary Time, The Solemnity of Christ the King,

The First Sunday of Advent. In the poverty of the hospital room, I would sometimes see the heavens opened, and the visual drabness of the room become the splendor of the heavenly liturgy, all because one humble priest thought enough of his priesthood to extend it to me on the Lord's Day. Together, we would join the rest of the Body of Christ and so enter into the unity of the church celebrating the Eucharist from the rising of the sun to its setting. After a breakfast of pancakes from the cafeteria, he would return to his parish in time for the later Masses, and I would sink back into the sameness that was also the fullness.

For the rest, my hermit life, to the extent that the continual hospital routine would allow it, continued with its strong, sweet smell, difficult at first to tolerate but so refreshing when fully inhaled. Otherwise, my schedule was punctuated by daily cell phone contact with the Mepkin community. But even these conversations only served to isolate me further by highlighting the ambiguity of my situation: the lack of control, and no estimation of the length of the hospital stay, no guarantees, nothing solid on which to base my life for the foreseeable future. And so many things seemed to be hanging over my head, especially the care of the community.

At the end of November, with my temperature still well over a hundred degrees on most days, the doctor had a long consultation with me and said, "We are not doing you any good in here. I am convinced that you have a bacteriological infection somewhere in your body that we cannot seem to find. It may be an infection you contracted during your travels. It may be coming from your lungs. It may yet be tuberculosis. But you are not exhibiting any signs of cancer, even though, given your stomach problems and fevers, you seem to have symptoms of transformed disease, that is, the CLL has transformed into lymphoma. Some on my staff are convinced of this, but I cannot be, since the scans show no new nodes with any significant cancer growth. Lymphoma always shows these. And if we treat you with chemotherapy, and you do not have lymphoma, but an infection, we will end up killing you even as we are trying to help you. So I am going to let you go, with the proviso that you stay in the area for a week or so, come see me and we will determine where we go from there."

I assumed, through no logical reasoning, that when I got out of the hospital, I would begin to recover, that the fevers would go down, that I would be able to return to the routine so long established. I obeyed the doctor and stayed in the area at a hotel paid for by a close friend and benefactor of the monastery who was insistent that I get out of the hospital and get some real rest before returning to Mepkin. At my next visit to the doctor things did not change. He agreed to let me return to South Carolina, but I would have to see him again before Christmas. So I returned home, and a joyful return it was. I was filled with the hope of a full recovery after my long hospital stay. But I had very little to back up that expectation.

In the days that followed, and in the space of reflection, I knew that I had had a brush with God, a new kind of experience where almost everything had been turned off in my spiritual life except the time alone, gazing at the mystery. That invitation always remains, even now, yet I cannot respond to it at will. The grace to do that had come with the hospital stay. The nothingness of all things had become the source of life for all things, when I let God enter the emptiness of fasting, the withdrawal from easy conversation, the fasting from reading, and the fasting from the familiar. What opened was the narrow gate of suffering, the loss of almost everything, including so much of human dignity and reserve, which I experienced in the hospital. Suffering at the invitation of God, I concluded, admits into us a new life and a warmer love. Long had I been preparing for this. Long had I dreamed about it. Now, it had been mine, only not mine but given as an invitation in the most unlikely of desert places, a semi-private hospital room. To try to make sense of it, to consider that this unpleasantness was all worth it for the sake of wisdom and spiritual experience is to misunderstand it entirely. I was not paying for anything. The suffering was precisely the dying of many parts of me, and the resistance and even refusal of it which coursed through my veins. But I always remembered that, as much as Jesus must have resisted, the church applies to him this text in the Scriptures, ". . . he did not open his mouth; like a lamb that is led to the slaughter, and like a sheep that before its shearers is silent, so he did not open his mouth" (Is. 53:7bc). In the course of being led away, one comes to understand that it is useless to complain before God; that his will, operative at every moment if only we have the senses to perceive it, hovers so close to us as to drown out our childlike fears and dread. He is always there. He is never absent. When nothing makes sense to us, we are invited to remember how deep is his call through this physical world. Yet, we dare not make it our end, for the physical world is his doorway into the fullness of being and communion for which we long in music, art and poetry. God not only offers this intimacy, he gives it to us in the following of Christ. But it is only in faith that we can imitate the Christ who remained silent before his accusers, even if he cried out to his Father in prayer to deliver him from the chalice of pain.

Even when I was back home at Mepkin, I looked for the invitation of the lamb of suffering again and again. But I did not find it in the putting on of the familiar. For it was only to be given in the intensive straitjacket of the cancer that was enveloping me.

Back in New York, right before Christmas, I underwent yet another HIV test, a tuberculosis test (which was to take several months while the cultures for finding this bacteria matured) and more scans. Everything continued to show up negative. The doctor let me go home for Christmas and I resumed my duties.

By Christmas Eve, I was suffering high fevers and severe dehydration. I had a glass of water by me at the Presider's Chair during the First Mass of Christmas. I got through the ceremony, but with dread that my almost constant sweating would damage the handmade gold vestment and that I would faint with stomach pain. My answer to all of this was to force myself to keep moving, keep fulfilling the duties expected of me. But, as the liturgies of Christmas proceeded, I knew I was sick. Yet, I could not find God as I had found him in the hospital room. All I could find was this increasing illness and the seeming demands of the season, both liturgical and pastoral. On Christmas night, I was eating supper alone in the refectory, preparing for the Third Mass of Christmas which we celebrate in the evening. So bad was the stomach pain that I got up from the bench and began pounding the walls in desperation. I no longer cared who saw or heard me. I was close to my end. The day after Christmas was a Sunday. I was with a distinguished visitor, Fr. Ladislas Orsy, SJ, a dear friend of the community and a close personal friend. He had come to my room in the senior wing, that part of the monastery where the older and sick monks are cared for. This was now my abode. During our visit, I began feeling very sick, both from stomach pain and nausea. I asked him to leave, so that I could be sick in the bathroom. The nurse, David George, visiting for Christmas, came in and examined me and wanted to take me to the local hospital for IV fluids. I refused, for on the natural and human level I wanted no more of that suffering now that I was home again and returning to what I hoped would be a normal life. He insisted that I go, for he could arrange for a private bed in the ER where I could get what I needed and come home. I agreed and, without clothes, toothbrush or anything else, we set out for the hospital. When we got there, his plan of anonymity began well enough. Then, an intrusive doctor came in and insisted that he examine me. What with my fever, low blood counts and now pneumonia, he would not let me go home. I refused his treatment. He argued with me for fifteen minutes, and crying and screaming inside, I was hospitalized once again, this time in Charleston. I knew that they would find nothing, no signs of growing cancer, no infection, no grave illness, yet here I was fading away without a clear diagnosis. I proved to be right about the diagnosis, though the medical team was most sympathetic. Their guess was my gallbladder as the probable cause of the fevers. After the pneumonia cleared up, they proceeded to order another complete GI workup, an ultrasound of my gallbladder, and, of course, more scans. Determined to beat this, I pleaded with the doctor as the tests came back negative, one by one, to let me out on New Year's Eve, that if MSKCC could not find the cause of the fevers and sweats, and he couldn't either, then let medical science be dumb on this one and allow me to continue my life as best I could with the cloudy diagnosis, "fever of unknown origin." My temperature on New Year's Eve was 103 degrees.

I returned to the monastery, confused but ready to try to keep living the monastic life and to be the Abbot of the monastery. No one could help me, no one knew what it felt like to have a raging fever that spiked at least twice a day and then broke with four or five hours of debilitating sweats that required constant change of clothes, underwear and bedsheets. In the few days that ensued, I took to the bed in the empty room next to me during the night, just to get dry for a few hours. Since there was no sleep possible during the sweats, I was growing exhausted and my stomach was refusing food. I called our Generalate in Rome and told Dom Timothy Kelly, the Procurator General, that I could not seem to get medical help anywhere, that I decided merely to stay at Mepkin, assume a reduced schedule, and see if my body would heal itself. After all, perhaps the whole thing was in my head, and that this was a massive breakdown after too many years of overwork. That's how delusional I had become. That's how far along the road of confusion this suffering had brought me. I could no longer reason properly. I could no longer get a sense of the reality of things. I was descending into a vortex of God's doing. Helpless, I simply acquiesced. No prayers, No devotion. No insight. No clarity. Only the experience of physical diminishment and loss.

The community could take no more of my graying condition. They went to David George and told him that something must be done with the doctor in New York. David called the doctor and said, "This man is dying in front of us. Can you do something?" The doctor, immediately on hearing of the increased symptoms, prescribed massive doses of Prednisone and told David to get me on the first plane to New York. Through generous friends, Larry and Beth Burtschy, I was able to get a flight on a private corporate jet. Alone on the flight, I felt once again the growing withdrawal from all things familiar and beloved. But here I was back in New York, a city where I had lived, studied and worked, a city that I had left to enter the monastery but where I was now being drawn back in some kind of awful paradox of inclusion. I proceeded to the hospital and was admitted for more tests and for chemotherapy treatment. This time the tests gave the doctor what he wanted—a welter of very cancerous nodes all across the abdomen. He was satisfied that what he was treating was a case of transformed disease, or lymphoma.

Back in the hospital for almost two weeks before treatment began, I had time to experience all over again the emptiness of loss and the fullness of God's presence in the nothingness. At Mepkin, a group of Members of Congress, gathered by the Faith and Politics Institute in Washington, gathered at the monastery without me. Later in January, the Board of Cistercian Publications, in its alliance with Liturgical Press and Western Michigan University, of which I am the chair, also traveled to Mepkin and I could not be there. I knew that God would take care of these meetings, that without my presence some greater good would come of their gatherings, and that the important thing for me to do was to allow others in the monastic community to look after things, which they did most capably with Fr. Aelred Hagan as the Prior.

In evidence, too, this time was the monastic resolve I had known earlier. I had a series of roommates, both sweet and bitter. The never-ending TV could sometimes be replaced by the silence of a like-minded person who cherished the solitude and quiet afforded by a sympathetic roommate. But most of the time this boon would be followed by the opposite, someone who lived all day, and sometimes all of the night, with the TV on as if it were some kind of drug not to be lived without. Great sadness comes over me when I consider the inanity of much of TV viewing. Even if I could not see the screen, I could hear the dialogue and the endless, meaningless music, the ever-repeated commercials, and the banal chatter of sitcoms and talk shows. And at night, the flashing and changing screen would pop over the curtain and dance on the wall beside me, like a temptation from the Life of St. Anthony of the Desert.

Chemotherapy treatment began in the middle of January and was repeated every three weeks for a series of six treatments. The regimen called for was the traditional R-CHOP, a long-tested combination of drugs prescribed for a number of cancers. The effects are severe: nausea, hair loss, fatigue, etc. Yet these were mitigated by large doses of Prednisone, which also has the effect of breaking down muscle tissue, firing up one's appetite, and leaving one bloated. I had an excess of all of these. But I felt well enough after the first treatment in the hospital to be released and receive the other treatments as an outpatient. I was told to stay in the New York area, so as to come back for booster shots and checkups for another two treatments. So determined was I to keep a good schedule and continue development work for the monastery while in New York, that I often arranged a dinner or meeting on the day of the five- to six-hour chemotherapy infusion. My angel of light, Kate Sullivan, would stay with me during treatment and then install me on the couch of her boss's office for a half hour or so in order to get nausea and other side effects under control. Then, I would proceed to my appointment.

"I have become like a pelican in the wilderness, like an owl in desolate places" (Ps. 101[102]:7). For the subsequent two treatments, I was invited and accepted to stay with Msgr. Philip J. Franceschini in his parish on Staten Island. He offered a welcoming and gracious atmosphere, with a most friendly group of brother priests, especially Fr. John Mercer, and a devoted staff, especially the cook, Chiara, who is from Rome and provided the kind of Italian cooking I had so enjoyed when I was a student there in the early 80s. The occasional bouts of nausea and debilitating fatigue could always be dealt with in this caring place. And the maturity of the priests and the people comforted me in my very changing physical circumstances. Here, I was alone in the suite of rooms they offered me, but I was not alone since they were always at hand to go for a walk, or to go for a drive, or just to talk. To the Monsignor, I owe such a great debt of gratitude that I feel I could never adequately repay it. I shall never forget his offer, indeed, his demand, to take care of the management of the dozens of pills I had to take during this time. This, and many other services he rendered me, has made him a brother and I love him for it.

During my time on Staten Island, I came to a better understanding of my situation. How much I missed the monastery, the brethren, the way of life there, welled up in my mind and into tears when I would walk in Willowbrook Park, just a few blocks away from the rectory. The oak forest in winter, frozen pond, homeless geese, a smattering of cars of those few who could stand the cold, all mirrored back to me how I felt—barren, deprived, an exile, a person without resources. All of this weighed in on my hope and gave it a new definition. There was nothing left to hope for of the things I once knew. Even those whom I served were gone from me. I could no longer render Gospel service to them. All I had was this illness and now the treatment for it, which even took away the body I once possessed. Back to the rectory I would return from my walk, now dry-eyed but sober and ready to experience what the next moment or hour might bring. But it would not be my actions or my work. I was now passive to something else to which I could give no name, but which I had learned to trust and even to feel comfortable in. When some strength returned right before the next treatment, I would attempt to play the organ. The skill was still there, but my fingers tingled and grew numb at the tips, and my feet felt like pounds of hard rubber. No elasticity and no amount of work seemed to loosen them up. I could no longer play with any comfort, and in my present condition I had no desire to. Once my form of prayer, and one of the greatest gifts I had known from the Lord, was now gone with no realistic chance of getting it back. The effect of the one drug causing these symptoms could last for a year or more. For the foreseeable future, I was without music. Nor did I have the desire to listen to music. Sometimes at night, when I could not sleep, and this was frequently the case, I would "play" through whole symphonies or concertos and rise and fall with the drama of the music. But this was like counting sheep. It was the activity the least offensive to the call of pure prayer. It was certainly better than reading, walking, or even talking in the face of the wealth of the empty space and silence that was offered during a sleepless night. I learned that even the imagination of music was to be jettisoned in favor of something else far richer but which I could not really describe. I reasoned that with so much music in my head, with so much in my memory, I had no need of listening, of filling my mind and heart with things I already know and have experienced, or things that now seemed to lessen the purity of the nothingness of my landscape.

". . . in the shadow of your wings I rejoice. My soul clings to you; your right hand holds me fast" (Ps. 62[63]:8b-9). After two more treatments, three weeks apart, I returned to Mepkin and South Carolina. For the remaining three treatments, I would return briefly to New York. I rejoiced in seeing the brethren, of resuming a light schedule, though I could not attend the night office. I needed too much sleep. I didn't mind the surprise at and the remarks on my physical condition, moon faced and heavy. I didn't care, so much was I having to deal with. By the late spring and early summer, with the treatments over and a time of recovery at hand, I prepared to resume my work. But it was never quite the same. I still had to rest in the afternoons. I felt that I was performing my pastoral duty, and I was setting in motion some long-delayed projects around the monastery. But practicing the organ or piano was a chore, even though I could get enthusiastic about this or that musical project. Somehow, I was not myself. I walked much more slowly, could not summon energy at will, or rise easily to the occasion of being an extrovert.

Some in the community thought me depressed by my illness. But I knew that this was not the case. I was saddened at another loss, that of the silvery nothingness which had been filled with mystery, a mystery I knew to be God. I felt that I was in some kind of twilight, neither here nor there, neither begun nor finished, in the world but not of it, compromised forever because I had suffered so much loss, and, yet, here it was all back again, but not quite. The doctor had told me that I could expect to be lymphoma free for perhaps fifteen or sixteen years. I would still have the CLL to deal with and, though not curable, usually able to be treated. In this new dryness and shadow, I would have to go the richer and the poorer for what I had experienced.

"But you, O Lord . . . how long? Return, Lord, rescue my soul. Save me in your merciful love" (Ps. 6:4b-5a). So the summer wore on. And then, as if it had been pre-ordained and somehow predicted, my symptoms of sweats, mounting fever and stomach pain gradually returned. At first I was in denial. The doctor thought that the nausea and gagging I was having were in my head, a reaction to a new medication to steady my lowering white blood cell counts. I knew better. But I could not get myself to believe that the cancer was back. These symptoms must be something new, I thought. But I also felt I was being stalked by something very unpleasant and dreadfully familiar. By September, I was having nightly bouts with sweats and daily bouts with fevers. Sometimes, the sweats would continue during the day, and the fevers kept getting higher and higher and extending into the night.

When I visited the doctor in the third week of September, and after more tests, he made an immediate plan for hospitalization and a new round of chemotherapy. Surprised, disappointed and alarmed, he told me that mine was an unusual case. Would I accept "investigational chemo," something that he and his research associates had developed for this kind of recurrence? Yes, I would. I wanted to fight for life, but around the corner, I thought, lay something bigger than both me and the doctor and all his science. And that was the will of God, which was once again lowering down upon me with its cloud of suffering. Inside, I fought, twisted and turned. I begged the doctor for at least a week more at Mepkin to finish business, wrap up affairs with the brothers and receive my entire family who were once again on their way for their annual visit. Not again could I leave so abruptly. Not again would I be so absent from the familiar. But my last week at home was filled with visits to the local clinic for infusions and the like, for by that time I had no immune system. The fevers and sweats continued, and they rendered me useless and very sick. I should have stayed in New York as the doctor had wished. I seemed to be two persons, one straining to hang on to Mepkin, the other called to the adventure of passive but illuminative experience. Being cared for and held in sympathy by my brothers in community and constantly assured of prayers by friends and well-wishers, I readied myself for the rugged experience I suspected was in store for me.

What I did not know was that this time there would be no Prednisone to soften the effects of the new chemo. There would be no traveling back and forth between treatments to South Carolina, for this new chemo was far too strong and the side effects too debilitating for travel. I would have to stay in New York for at least the first three treatments, and these a month apart. I had already been in the hospital two weeks for tests before treatment to see if my system was strong enough to tolerate the poison. This time the brothers insisted that someone from the community be with me, especially during the treatments, to help with meals and other care. Father Stanislaus and Sr. Bridget Sullivan, a good friend of the community and a close personal friend, came to New York and arranged for my assistance. They procured an apartment across the street from the hospital, and to here I would return between treatments once they started. During all this time, I was consoled by frequent visits of the brothers who would care for me during the time of treatments. The retired Bishop of Charleston, David B. Thompson, also cared for me by his frequent telephone calls, as well as my dear friend, Msgr. James A. Carter of Charleston, who visited me and gifted me with his presence, as well as many others.

I found that the treatments were bad enough, but that my white blood cell counts were so low that I began to catch a series of opportunistic infections that sent me back to the hospital four times during the first three treatments. And here is where I gazed into the bottom of suffering.

"Many dogs have surrounded me, a band of the wicked beset me. They tear holes in my hands and my feet and lay me in the dust of death" (Ps. 21[22]:17). The infections that plagued me during this period made me so sick that in a space of four or five hours I would become so frightened at my condition of nausea, fevers, chills, etc., that I gladly obeyed the doctor when he said I must come to the hospital with a fever over 100.5 degrees. But back in the hospital, I was faced once again with the discipline of the roommate and would have to turn to the Rule of St. Benedict and the Sermon on the Mount for sustenance. During each of these four hospitalizations, the demons seemed to come out of the walls. The "sticks" that now occurred were so painful that I felt myself taken beyond my threshold of endurance and thrust into fear. As I was being prepared for yet another CT scan, the IV nurse could not find a vein. Even after hot compresses on my arm so as to reveal a vein, the sticking continued without success. I could take no more. I wept and lifted up my heart and mind to God, and what I found was Christ crucified, and not my pain any longer, but his. Could this be some kind of union? Though still in agony, I knew that I was comforted, not physically but spiritually, because I was privileged to be at that kenosis that saves us all. It was only a brief taste of it, yet I was there by invitation and careful preparation during all these months. I am grateful, but I am wary of the next invitation, should that come.

And it did. Recently, after yet another hospitalization, I spoke to one of the nurse practitioners, who told me the fate of my first roommate, a young Filipino named Michael. He had been almost constantly hospitalized since the end of 2004. His family distraught, they had arranged for trips to Lourdes and other pilgrimage places to pray for a cure. But the young man had never been able to go, since his low platelet count could not counter his almost constant infections. The nurse practitioner told me that Michael said finally no more to the antibiotics that would narrowly save him from an overwhelming infection. He succumbed in July of 2005. And now, I would at last glimpse what seemed to be a leukemia death right in the same room with me. My roommate had acute leukemia and had been treated with chemotherapy in preparation for a bone marrow transplant. A young, big, strapping fellow of 45, he seemed to need no treatments. But his counts were low, and his immune system awash. He was receiving his medication and having his blood drawn by a MediPort, so he was saved the painful inconvenience of the "sticks." His girlfriend was in close attendance in the partition next to me. One night his fever began to mount, and his blood pressure dropped—a sure sign of a growing infection. The doctors suspected the MediPort as the source of infection. The girlfriend became alarmed as did the nurses. Immediately came in the oxygen and the fluids that would try to steady his system and drive back the sepsis infection that was about to take him. So much equipment meant that the curtain had to be drawn back, removing any privacy of this panic. The girlfriend started screaming. She came beside me in the bed and wept uncontrollably for a long time while the medical staff did their best. Soon, his lungs filled with the fluids. He began to hiccup to get the fluid out of his lungs, like a great beached whale. His blood pressure continued to drop and the fever was up to 105 degrees. There was nothing to do but wait and see who would win, he in his body or the infection. No one could tell. And the atmosphere of dread filled the room. The girlfriend jumped on his bed and shook him, shouting, "Don't you leave me!" And the agony of physical and emotional loss also crowded into the room. When all the emotion was spent and there was a kind of numb calm that went on for a few more hours, the big boy roused himself. The blood pressure began to rise, though the hiccups continued. The fever began to abate. He was not going to die, he was going to live, having found some kind of strength of will or grace of survival within himself. But the anatomy of the struggle was laid bare for all to see. I saw it and knew that this is the death that awaits me when it comes, if it should come with this cancer. I knew that a time arrives, between darkness and light, when one chooses to go on with the familiar or takes another invitation, if it is offered. I want to take the invitation, should it be offered. It will be offered some day, to me and to all of us. Yet, even in the familiar, we sometimes glimpse and hear the joy of the kingdom of God that awaits us at the end of the passage.

"My song is of mercy and justice; I sing to you, O Lord" (Ps. 100[101]:1). One day, appearing at the clinic for a checkup between treatments, I was called as usual into the phlebotomist's office to have my blood drawn. I had seen this woman before. She was as wide as she was high, with short hair, nicely arranged, that only emphasized her roundness. She was an immigrant, with a thick accent and very businesslike and formal. She was not someone easy for me to engage. On this particular day, I found nothing to engage me anyway. I was down, discouraged at this seemingly endless medical routine. I presented myself, looking glum and unsmiling. She took my cue immediately and said very slowly, "You no look happy. You don't get well unless you are happy. What iss wrong with you?" Intrigued, I said that today I was feeling low. She replied, "What iss dat ding on your neck?" She was referring to my Roman collar which I always wear when I come to the hospital as an outpatient. I said that I was a priest and a monk, and that I wore it as a sign of commitment to God. "But you have a Jewish name." Yes, I replied, but I was raised a Catholic and I did not know anything about my supposed Jewish origins. She grunted. Since I had gotten this far, I ventured to ask her about herself. "Where are you from?" I asked. "KiEFF. But day don like us dere. Day take our money, our apartments, our joy. So my fAAther and my mOOther, we decide to come here. But day don like us here either." She grunted again. "But we like you here," I replied, "and I might feel a lot better if you would sing me a song." Her eyebrows rose, and she put down her instruments. She splayed her hands and rolled from side to side, singing softly and in a gravelly alto a song from her childhood. She ended, offering both hands to me, and laughed the first laugh I had heard from her. I bolted up in the chair enthusiastically and told her how delighted I was. She continued, "My mOOther was sick. She could not walk. How we get her to train and on boat to come here? We don know what to do. One day, a wOOman with clothing all around her (and here she described with her hands what I took to be a veil and a wimple, though I was not yet sure) came to our house. She says to my fAAther, 'I can help your wife to walk better. Let her come with us for a week. Then she will come back to you stronger.' So my mOOther went with the wOOman." My nurse began to cry huge tears, even while the line of patients was piling up behind me, waiting their turn with her. With eyes wide and shining through tears, she said, "My mOOther, she come back, she not perfect, but she walk into our house. We took her to train. We got her on boat. We come here." And in her tears, she merely nodded to me, as if she really knew all about me and my kind, and that woman in Kiev who helped her mother. I, too, had to hold back tears, as I realized that this woman had found her tongue to celebrate once again a story that held a treasure in her life. And in that dingy room in the clinic, it came out of her. A moment of glory we had both realized, in the goodness of religious women, in their unsung actions for good, which today had been brought out of the treasure house and been brushed off not only for my benefit but, somehow, for the good of the church and the Jewish people represented by me and this woman from Kiev. I see her frequently in the hospital, and when we greet one another, we know.

"He said to him (Jesus), 'Teacher, I have kept all these (commandments) since my youth.' Jesus, looking at him, loved him and said, 'You lack one thing; go, sell what you own, and give the money to the poor, and you will have treasure in heaven; then come, follow me.' When he heard this, he was shocked and went away grieving, for he had many possessions" (Mk. 10:20-22). Not many days later, I returned to the day hospital for my second chemotherapy treatment. I had an early appointment with the doctor to make sure that I could be treated that day, since my blood counts several days earlier had been too low for treatment. The infusion takes more than four hours and I had no previous appointment in the day hospital. That means that after the doctor approves me for treatment, I must report to the day hospital, and wait several hours for the pharmacy to deliver the medication, and then wait perhaps for an indefinite time for a "chair" in which to receive it from a chemotherapy nurse. I had made a previous appointment to see my brother that evening at seven o'clock. I waited until almost four in the afternoon for treatment to begin. I was steaming with anger, as are many other patients who get caught in this situation, at this seeming waste of time and lack of organization in the day hospital where smiling attendants do their best to calm people down. I waited to vent my anger on the chemotherapy nurse. I lined my cryptic remarks with sugar so as not to give too much offense, but the young woman got my point. She apologized for the delay and acknowledged that the long wait must have been hard for me, and that she would do her best to speed things up. Even then, after all my monastic resolutions, I was still full of the possessions of control and righteousness. She chatted away as she prepared the IV line. Seeing the Roman collar, she asked if I were a priest. She went on to relate her own experiences of a legendary Catholic priest in Ecuador where she had been a medical volunteer. He had been a diocesan priest who had volunteered to join the Society of St. James which sends priests to Latin America for extended pastoral service to the poor. This particular priest was now in his nineties but still hale and hearty, and still serving in the sierra above Quito. I replied that I knew the area and had even heard of the priest. She was delighted and continued to fill in details of her life there and back here. Though she was not a Catholic, she greatly admired our faith and was considering a move to enter an RCIA program. We ended our conversation and the long treatment began. She would come back in periodically to check on and to change the series of five drugs. Way past seven o'clock, with my brother sitting in the chair beside me in the chemotherapy room, our evening ruined, the nurse returned to take out the IV line at the end of the treatment. She began to chat again, but this time there was a purpose to it. She told how she had administered chemotherapy to the poor mountain *indigenos* in Ecuador, how the medication was available but not the skill to counter its side effects. She went on to say how the mothers and fathers would bring their little ones to be treated and sometimes wait for a couple of days in the cold before the doctors and nurses could get to them. She narrated how sick they got, how pathetic it was to see children and adults vomiting and breaking out in rashes without the benefit of extra drugs to still the side effects. She ended by saying how fortunate we are in the States to have such sophisticated techniques for the reception of chemotherapy, and how little the time is that we have to wait in comparison to the poor. During her whole speech, she chatted away naturally, without any point of retribution or correction. I was cut to the quick. I got the point of her sword and it went right to my heart. For I knew Ecuador and its poor. Yet I could not transfer that poverty to my situation back in the States. Here, monk though I was who had given up everything, I was still rich. I had heard the call to be poor in the day hospital, but I had turned it down in order to stay rich. I have told this story to many people to show my own spiritual poverty. And I continue to admire that nurse, who was so kind as not to correct me with bitterness or sternness, but, who, nevertheless, knew what her duty was toward me.

"I have sunk into the mud of the deep and there is no foothold. I have entered the waters of the deep and the waves overwhelm me" (Ps. 68[69]:3). Another lesson awaited me in the next hospitalization. Wheeled into the room late at night, with a high fever and symptoms of nausea, chills and severe headache, I heard beyond the curtain a high-pitched male voice shouting into a cell phone food orders in great quantities. To whom? To where? Business at midnight? Every light in his partition was ablaze. No light was needed in my part of the room. It was like living in night baseball. I was revolted, and grew angry, and could not sleep because of it, sick as I was. It was not the bother of the lights and the voice, it was the stupidity of it, the lack of courtesy, the inhumanity and the disdain for other people. Eventually I slept and was careful the next morning not to disturb him, who snored all through the day and repeated the same performance the next night. By this time, I was out of sorts and my thoughts were ugly. I could not find it within me to tolerate this ignorance. I could not find my discipline. I could not conquer the situation. I had to relent to my weakness and let the Spirit of God do in me what I manifestly could not do. After all I had been through, I was still so intolerant. I had met my match, and a slime which blotted out my light oozed over me. Gone was my monasticism, gone was my observance. I was like so many others, at war with myself and my surroundings. My fortress had finally been completely overrun. It took a few hours, the Scriptures, and God's love to show me that God had taken me down, and that he had crushed my fortress by his power. This Haitian next to me was only the instrument of God's assault, as the Egyptians were for the Israelites at the Red Sea, and as the Babylonians and the Persians were for the Jews. God was now teaching me his most precious lesson.

I introduced myself to the Haitian the second morning. It was as if I was not the one who was speaking, but someone else was speaking through me. For my feelings were not in tune with my actions. He was charming to speak with, even if his demands of the nurses continued and his bawling into the cell phone never ceased through two or three in the morning. After all, he was suffering worse than I was, with lymphoma in the neck, which gave him a constant cough and necessitated ICE chemotherapy, which he received in the hospital for three days every month. After speaking with him, I realized that here was another human being groping for the light. He had not much in the way of consideration of others, but he extended a gracious welcome to me and then told me, when he realized that I was a monk, of his charitable activities for the poor in Africa. He even gave me a $5 calling card for Africa. It was to there, six hours ahead of us, that his calls were made after midnight. Wider must my net grow, I thought. Larger must my tolerance stretch. For there are some who, while exhibiting an excellent courtesy, do very little for others. Yet, we maintain a pleasant relation with them because they are civil. While others, lacking sophistication, enlarge their hearts and actions in love to their neighbor, and it is up to us to appreciate their worth. The Haitian was discharged before me. But before he was gone, I made my peace with the bright lights, even after he was asleep and snoring, for he never turned them out. I made peace with his noise and the reckless requests. I made peace. I learned that there are no limits to suffering, that is, to what I do not like. No limits to perceived affronts, to suspected lack of courtesy or respect. No matter how much one is trained in the school of tolerance, it remains a mystery in what it still may ask. There are simply no limits to it. That is my definition of suffering. But in the meantime, one learns a depth of the human heart and a knowledge not found in books. Eventually, I left the hospital much chastened, with a new heart and a mind refreshingly liberated.

Epilogue. "I am hard pressed between the two: my desire is to depart and be with Christ, for that is far better; but to remain in the flesh is more necessary for you" (Phil. 1:23-24). I remain sick and listen to the doctor's medical hopes and expectations with ears not cynical but wise. I have seen too much, been through too much. If I recover, I will not be the same. I will not look back on the "bad days" as something past and over with. I would not want that, not after what I have seen and heard. Perhaps this experience will be an illuminative presence throughout the rest of a longer life. If so, it will take years to digest, even though its fresh details are better recorded now, without mature reflection. This much I know, that in the mystery of suffering one comes against one's limits on many fronts. But one also can open the door to a communion with as many divine dimensions or more than the experience. The pain, of whatever kind, is the key to opening the door. It makes us need God, who wants to be needed. It momentarily reveals to us our dependency on our Creator, who wants only too much to grow in intimacy with us through our need of him. "Give us this day our daily bread." It builds endurance and character. It creates a new kind of hope, based solidly on his love for us and for others. Then the other becomes like one of our family, and we are always ready to do the most for them. The question of who is our neighbor becomes moot. All are our neighbors. Everyone. Barriers fall, prejudices shrink, opportunities appear, when we love the neighbor and offer love when he is temporarily out of his wits, or when she has for the moment forgotten her dignity. Love insists on the noble, sees through to the essential, ignores the ugly, intuits the beautiful, deflects the violence from its own destructive blindness and waits for its redirection for the good.

But it could also be that God has spoken definitively through this cancer, and I am on my way to him shortly. The only way forward is to wait on God, and continue to endure, for that is what our life is, in union with Christ. Perhaps it is better for me to stay here and proclaim God's goodness to my neighbors. But I long, as we all do, for that upward call of God in Christ Jesus. I wait anxiously for the day to accept the invitation that will come to take the hand God offers and go through the door of death.

New York City
Christmas Eve, 2005

ESSAY III

Desire

*"O God, you are my God, for you I long;
for you my soul is thirsting."* (Ps. 62[63]:2ab)

Introduction. Desire that is lifelong is rare. We have many desires which, when satisfied, wither and fade from memory. Corrupt desires tend to grow with intensity and swallow up all in their path, even going so far as to greatly diminish us who desire them. But they cannot destroy the person because we come from the creative touch of God. Desires that are inordinate merely feed on an infinite hunger from a finite source. They themselves will die when we die. Yet our desire for God, when it is recognized and nourished throughout life, continues even after death. God calls us first by his creation of us and then by his own desire to have a relationship with us. The call comes, for the most part, through his Word in his church. We respond and God responds again in a kind of reciprocity. We are intrigued and move further toward God. We are fascinated by God's attraction. We want to know where "he (Jesus) lives" (Jn. 1:38), that is, how we can know his teaching, his way of life, and his person. We keep moving in God's direction, sometimes with great speed, sometimes slowly. But there comes a point when he seems to disappear. We grope for his presence, we twist and turn in his absence. We are caught in the net of his own design. He can be so palpably, tangibly real. He can also withdraw as quickly and as absolutely as he was concrete a moment ago.

God's grace works in sundry ways. Some are drawn along with just enough spiritual nourishment to keep them on a fidelity track with God. Others experience an exciting spiritual moment, perhaps for a year or two, before the light goes out; God seems absent, and they forget him. This essay is about those who manage to keep going on the spiritual path. Their desire may have passed into a low flame of daily fidelity. Their work for the kingdom is manifold and fruitful, though, in the daily routine, they tend not to see its outcome. They acknowledge the necessity of spiritual reading and exercise to keep the hearth embers of the love of God aglow. But they find themselves always searching for the one spirituality or method that will lift them out of their malaise.

Families find themselves much taken up with the rearing of their children. This monumental Christian work, in and of itself, keeps them on a steady spiritual journey. Yet, the Gospel keeps calling mothers and fathers all through the rapid transition stages of family experience. The children cannot be the objects of their spiritual search. God beckons them out of being mere biological, social and economical parents into a further vocation of being a life-giving family, guiding and counseling adolescents and young adults in the ways of Christianity. Can the church provide for them the fire and the flame of Gospel desire?

Though our culture is shot through with the presence of God, for God is everywhere calling individuals to himself, it is, nevertheless, full of attitudes, structures and postures that go blatantly contrary to the Gospel. As God makes his call to us, and as we try to respond, a close attention to the Gospel teaching, even against the current cultural tide, is often the way forward. Once one has thirsted for the Gospel, one has undertaken a long, contentious journey. We struggle with the discernment of right and wrong. We agonize over the choices that appear so clear on the one hand, and so cloudy on the other. At times, the choices are not between perceived good things and bad but between two goods. Which is more salient? To which is God calling us? Only a heart chastened by desire can begin to make sense out of these conundrums. God's way often lies hidden behind what seems foolish and overly generous. Only a mind and heart in tune with his can follow him.

The church can get so caught up in its pastoral and missionary work that it forgets or neglects the desire for God. Only adherence and love of the Scriptures can correct this sad tendency. When the desire for God grows cold in the hardness of routine, tradition, and daily work, only an unexpected and severe compunction of heart can loosen it. Where can we find this intensity of love for God in the church? Is it to be found only on yearly retreats, when resolutions fade within the first week of return to the familiar? Is it to be found in methods of prayer, insights which bleach yellow as the pages do on which they were first written ten years before? Is it to be discovered in new programs and policies based on social truths or ephemeral spiritualities? Or is it to be found within the church itself where the Spirit has poured out on faithful hearts the gifts of prayer, ascetic living and Gospel desire? These gifts stand stored in treasure houses too deeply hidden for most in the church to find. The task of cleaning and restoring these objects seems too arduous. Yet, here lies the answer to the question of the desire for God. The monastic tradition stands guard at the door of this treasure house. It is time for the church to rediscover the contemplative monastic tradition, even as monks and nuns begin to discover their own heritage. In so doing, the church will reconnect so many of its devotions and spiritualities to the one desire for God. Through the concept of the desire for God, the contemplative monastic tradition holds the key to Gospel living, not only in ancient times but in our time as well.

"Listen carefully, my son, to the master's instructions, and attend to them with the ear of your heart" (RSB Prol. 1). Right at the beginning of Ordinary Time in the liturgical year, the church assigns readings in each of the three cycles on God's call to us. In Cycle B in the First Book of Samuel at chapter three, God calls the young boy Samuel who is lying down in the temple of the Lord. The Lord calls him three times and each time the boy does not know that it is the Lord. He goes to Eli, the priest of the Lord, whom he assumes is calling him. After the third time, Eli realizes that the voice Samuel hears is God's voice. He counsels the boy, "Go, lie down; and if he calls you, you shall say, 'Speak, Lord, for your servant is listening'" (1 Sam. 3:9b). This is the insight the church wishes to impart at the very beginning of this cycle of readings. To listen to the Lord is the fundamental stance and

attitude for the spiritual journey. The monastic tradition, synthe-
sized by the Rule of St. Benedict, begins with the admonition to
listen. The voice of the Lord, as with Samuel, can often go dis-
guised as something else. By listening carefully, and not just with
the mind, but also with the heart, one can begin to discern God's
call. Many other noises compete with God's voice. Yet, God keeps
up his incantation until we are convinced in our whole being that
he is calling us.

God's call goes to the center of one's being and is perceived
to be totally personal. It belongs to no one else. It finds a ground
of being in us that we recognize as only our own. No one else
should know of it. No one else could understand it. Quiet and
calm accompany this first stirring of God in us. We walk around
in our social circle the same, but not the same. We are different,
but not in a way that can be perceived by others or described to
them as yet. Though we may be baptized and openly affiliated
with a parish in the church, this call seems to be summoning us
out of the ordinary and into a personal relationship with God,
perhaps for the first time since our childhood experience.

Though we may think that we are the ones who have awak-
ened to God's voice, and that it is our goodness and virtue that
have empowered us to listen, we should consider the Scriptures
which remind us that we are sinners, that is, unwilling and afraid
to hear the voice of the Lord. After Adam and Eve had eaten of
the forbidden fruit, the Lord called to Adam, "Where are you?"
Adam replied, "I heard the sound of you in the garden, and I was
afraid, because I was naked; and I hid myself." God said, "Who
told you that you were naked? Have you eaten from the tree of
which I commanded you not to eat" (Gen. 3:9-11)? From this fear
of God and from the attitude of not wishing to listen, lest one
hears words of shame and correction, comes all of the sorrow of
the world and its violence. Afraid of listening to God, we pass
to other voices we think will be more pleasing and affirming. We
listen only long enough to get what we want, and we proceed to
fill the world with our speech—speech to ourselves, to others, to
anyone or anything so as to drown out the emptiness where that
one voice we dread so much to hear can be heard. To listen to
God's voice may be the most frightening thing we ever do.

But God makes his voice appealing. He overcomes our sin,
shame, and fear by awakening our desire. The voice of the Lord

most frequently finds a way into our sympathies by the death of Christ. St. Paul makes the case for the initiative of God. "But God proves his love for us in that while we still were sinners Christ died for us" (Rom. 5:8). It is God in Christ who first calls us through the grace of our Baptism into a new and personal relationship with him. In Christ, gone are the recriminations of the Law and the guilt of the inevitable sinner. Gone is the fear that God is someone who cannot know us or our suffering. Instead, we hear the voice of one who beckons, not sweetly, not hesitatingly, but with power and authority.

The voice of God is startling and attractive. The disciples of John the Baptist stand and watch Jesus pass by. John proclaims him the "Lamb of God" (Jn. 1:36). The disciples leave John and follow Jesus. Jesus turns and says to them, "What are you looking for?" They ask, "Rabbi (which translated means Teacher), "where are you staying?" Jesus says to them, "Come and see" (Jn. 1:38). The disciples of John the Baptist represent the whole of the desire of Israel for God. The Psalmist voices this desire throughout the psalter: "My soul is ever consumed as I long for your decrees" (Ps. 118[119]:20). Though the Word of God is full of justice and judgment against human failings and infidelity, it continues to attract Israel, through which Israel was formed as a people and a nation. Once the Word of God has been taken into Israel, the Israelites must proclaim God's glory and grandeur. The prophet Jeremiah describes the Word of God in the mouth of the Israelites: "For the word of the Lord has become for me a reproach and derision all day long. If I say, 'I will not mention him, or speak any more in his name,' then within me there is something like a burning fire shut up in my bones; I am weary with holding it in, and I cannot" (Jer. 20:8c-9). The disciples of John the Baptist sense that passing before them is the one who holds the answer to all their questions about the Law, the Prophets, and the Psalms, shut up in their bones like a burning fire. They believe that they have found the Messiah. They wish to come and see the whole teaching of the one declared to be the Lamb of God.

The Word of God sustains us for the length of a journey we have no mind of nor cannot know. It reveals itself to be a journey of desire. In order to take the next step along this journey, the spiritual person must turn to prayer. By prayer, one's desire is strengthened and supported. The time will come when the prayer of the faithful one grows weary of ever reaching its goal. The more specific and noble the intention, the more God tests our desire. One thinks of St. Monica praying for the conversion of her son, Augustine. The wife's desire that her husband stop drinking or the husband's desire that his wife come back home are both examples of how focused our prayer can become and how purifying. The prayer of parents for a wayward child may stretch out for years without result. Yet, the parents keep a wakeful heart before the throne of God. This urgent prayer may be a personal one for freedom from vice, sin, or unseemly habits. It may be a prayer during illness, which, in all the ambiguity of serious sickness, finally allows God to do whatever he wants. In all these cases, and in whatever other situations, the Scriptures teach us the proper attitude toward prayer. The psalter, the prayerbook of the church, may give words to our otherwise exhausted mind and heart. *Lectio Divina*, the prayerful reading of the Scriptures, may lend the support we need when prayer seems strained and difficult. Jesus' teaching in the Gospel of Luke, however, commands our attention.

After instructing his disciples in the prayer of the "Our Father," Jesus recounted the story of the persistent man who woke up the household of his friend at night. Though the man's friend did not get up out of friendship, he did rise and give the man what he wanted simply because he wouldn't give up. Persistence in prayer is Jesus' lesson. He continues with the unforgettable words, "Ask, and it will be given you; search, and you will find; knock, and the door will be opened for you" (Lk. 11:9). No one who gives up in prayer will obtain what they ask for. Their desire will grow cold.

Further on in the Gospel of Luke, Jesus addresses the question of prayer. "He told them a parable about their need to pray always and not to lose heart" (Lk. 18:1). The story tells of the importunate widow, who kept coming to the corrupt judge day and night. Because she was wearing him out with coming, and not because of the justice of her cause, the judge granted her justice. At this point, Jesus himself begins to interpret the parable. The kind of persistent prayer the widow engages in gradually transforms into a more pure prayer to God for justice of all sorts, not just one's own. Jesus asks, "And will not God grant justice to his chosen ones who cry to him day and night? Will he delay long in helping them?" (Lk. 18:7). But who, Jesus wonders, will be praying like this in the church when the Son of Man comes. Will God find anyone whose faith is strong enough to keep praying in the darkness?

The question remains in the church today. Who will remain in the stance of prayer beyond their own needs? Who will allow the Spirit to bring them to a place of pure prayer? We are not speaking here of methods of prayer and prayer postures. What is at stake is nothing less than the outbreak of the kingdom of God in the heart of the individual. How will that necessary purification come to us that leads beyond self-improvement, self-aggrandisement, spiritual ambition, and into poverty of spirit, the loss of supposed sanctity, the bending down of the arrogance of position, and the ceasing of human insistence in doing things my own way in power over others? The preparation for a more pure prayer before the Son of Man enters the hearts of those whose desire is kept alive by the constant living of the Gospel in its entirety and in its depth. No shallow embrace of God, no sickly agreement with him, will stand up under the fire of pure prayer. If one has not learned to live the Gospel according to the will of God for him or her, one is a pretender and will be cast out.

One looks for models for this kind of purification in the church. In the age of the first writers of Christianity, the widow exemplified the one who was the most needy, the one most forlorn in the patriarchal society of the day, the one most given to prayer alone, the one St. Augustine used so eloquently in his "Letter to Proba" on Christian prayer. In today's church, there rise up many new models. One thinks of the immigrant, the marginalized, the urban poor, the agricultural poor, and many more. Yet how many of these desire quite legitimately only for a better world for themselves and their families? How many take their desire to the new horizon of prayer for others and for all? How many are content to remain poor, outcast and scorned for the sake of the Gospel? Religious men and women have opened up new avenues of approach to prayer purification. Groups such as the Little Brothers and Sisters of Charles de Foucauld have found a way to identify with the poor, the outcast and the lonely for the sake of solidarity with those who thirst for justice. In this they pray to and with Jesus who thirsts for the faith of humankind and the bestowing of justice in his kingdom to come. Contemplative groups in the church (one thinks of the Poor Clares, Carmelites, Carthusians, Camaldolese, certain Benedictines, and others) have long borne the heat of the day in this kind of prayer at the heart of the church. The contemplative monastic tradition is by far the oldest and the richest in experience and attendant literature for the expression of pure prayer stemming from the deep desire for God. It is to this tradition we turn, not so much to illuminate the holiness of human desire so much as to enunciate something of the desire of God for us with which his Spirit burns as he touches us and raises up Christ in us. A spirituality of desire becomes a theology which identifies the Spirit as the desire of God. In living this burning desire of the Spirit, the contemplative monastic tradition may reclaim its necessary yet forgotten place in the minds and hearts of the faithful of our time.

"Tears have wasted my eyes, my throat and my heart. For my life is spent with sorrow and my years with sighs. Affliction has broken down my strength and my bones waste away" (Ps. 30[31]:10b-11). The figure of Mary Magdalene, the first to proclaim the resurrection, begins this study of the holiness of desire according to the contemplative monastic tradition. Whatever her story, mixed as it is with other women close to Jesus or at least converted to love him, she is presented in the Gospel of John as one who stood close by the cross of Jesus at his death. She heard his words to his mother, Mary, and to "the disciple whom he loved" (Jn. 19:25-26). After his body was taken away from the place of crucifixion and laid in the tomb of the garden where he was executed, Mary saw everything. She came back to the garden and the tomb as soon as it was religiously legal to do so, that is, very early on the first day of the week after the Sabbath. It was still dark. The stone had been removed from the tomb. Realizing with horror that he might have been stolen away, she ran at once to Simon Peter and the other disciple, "the one whom Jesus loved" (Jn. 20:2). The two disciples ran to the tomb to see what had happened. The other disciple, bowing to Simon Peter, held back at the tomb while he entered it and noted the details of the linen wrappings and the cloth that had been on Jesus' head. Then the other disciple went in, "and he saw and believed" (Jn. 20:8). The great grace of believing in the resurrection had been given to him, even though he did not predict it, for "as yet they did not understand the scripture, that he must rise from the dead. Then the disciples returned to their homes" (Jn. 20:9-10).

From this point on, Mary Magdalene becomes one of the preeminent models of the contemplative life. Her desire keeps her at the tomb when the others had left. They returned either to their ordinary routine or, more likely, to the circle of grieving disciples whom they had abandoned in sudden alarm at the news Mary had brought them. They resumed their cogitations over the Law and how the Messiah was to fulfill it. They will go on to become bishops, intellectuals, pastors and theologians, occupied with the practical matters of the nascent church and the pastoral questions of the day. But she was free enough and poor enough to remain. She had no career, no position in the church. We would project on her—and the many-layered Gospel of John invites us to do this—a withdrawal from all that is not directly Jesus. So particular had his call to her been, and so full her response, that she had bravely stood at the cross of Christ, and now she stood at the tomb weeping. She was empty so as to do nothing else than to mourn the loss of the one she had come to love with such a special force. She stood weeping not only for the loss of him whom she loved but also for her sins. We do not know if she had been a public sinner before her conversion to Christ. The Gospels of Mark and Luke declare that Christ had cast out of her seven demons (see Mk. 16:9; Lk. 8:2). But this may or may not influence the content of her weeping in the Gospel of John. Everyone drawn to an all-consuming love of Christ weeps for what still separates them from him, be it thoughts, or attitudes, or desires that may be unworthy of him. Her unworthiness, born from the recognition of his unconditional love for her, turns her grief to tears. And now the body is gone.

Mary bends down to look into the empty tomb. She sees two angels guarding the holy place of the resurrection. They ask her, "Woman, why are you weeping?" The question is well aimed, since the angels are appearing to her because of Christ's resurrection.

There can be no weeping at such a gift from God. Mary's tears are not yet those which the monastic tradition names as the gift of tears. These come in a combination of joy in Christ's victory, of gratitude for the gifts of the Spirit, and of sorrow for one's sins. Mary's tears are about the cutting of the ties of the love she had known.

Mary's tears may contain many elements of earthly possession, emotional attachment, passionate attraction, the love of beauty, the unconditional surrender of her person to her love. These, though most familiar to all of us, are of the earth and must undergo a transformation into the spiritual realm. The image they suggest of God's love and God's glory must die if they are to be redeemed. They cannot image adequately the transcendent glory of God who is spiritual. Without any doubt, they may bring people along the way for a time, but they are no substitute for the pure love of God, which is, at once, if not passionless, as some early writers suggested, then, jealous and all-desiring. Nothing, not even a glorious earthly image, not even a life taken up with the church's earthly matters, can brook the love of God. Mary's tears, however, contain the element that will redeem all the rest. In her admixtured love, there lies the seed of authentic spiritual desire planted in her by the Holy Spirit.

After Mary replies to the angels that the body of the Lord has been taken away to an unknown place, she turns and encounters Jesus, whom she does not recognize. Jesus, aiming more closely at the heart of Mary from whom he will require a great conversion, also asks her, "Woman, why are you weeping? Whom are you looking for?" (Jn. 20:13-15). The double question signifies a sympathy but also a challenge. Jesus means that there is no more reason to weep. He is there with her. But he also announces that the person she is looking for is there, but not there. He is raised from the dead and in that glory can no longer be recognized just as Jesus of Nazareth, but as the Christ, the victor over sin and death and the author of all life. This change will have profound spiritual consequences on her and on all of us as we make our journey forward to God.

Mary, supposing the man she has turned to face is the gardener, asks if he knows where the body of Jesus is. At this point, Jesus reveals himself to her, at once on familiar grounds, for he mentions her name but also in a completely new space that he will explain. When Mary hears her name, she turns again. But she had already turned to Jesus (see Jn. 20:14). Yet this is a new kind of turning where the human person stands in the face of divinity and yields its whole being to the God who now claims it. This is the same turning of the Israelites back to God:

> *For the Lord will again take delight in prospering you, just as he delighted in prospering your ancestors, when you obey the Lord your God by observing his commandments and decrees that are written in this book of the law, because you turn to the Lord your God with all your heart and with all your soul* (Dt. 30:9b-10).

In the opposite way, God prophesies against Israel that they will not turn to him and be faithful:

> *And he (the Lord) said (to Isaiah), "Go and say to this people: Keep listening but do not comprehend; keep looking, but do not understand." Make the mind of this people dull, and stop their ears, and shut their eyes, so that they may not look with their eyes, and listen with their ears, and comprehend with their minds, and turn and be healed* (Is. 6:9-10).

In the same way the Israelites beg the Lord to turn back to them:

> *God of hosts, turn again, we implore, look down from heaven and see. Visit this vine and protect it, the vine your right hand has planted* (Ps. 79[80]:15).

Mary turns to Jesus with her whole being: mind, heart, soul and body. She is ready to listen and to comprehend, to look and to understand, to make her mind acute and to unstop the ear of her heart. She opens her eyes to divinity and knows the world in a new way. Her whole being is turned from what had once been familiar to a new path, uncharted yet somehow bridged by the Spirit who elevates her love to the risen Christ.

Jesus moves the encounter to its clear and precise conclusion. He says to Mary, "Do not hold on to me, because I have not yet ascended to the Father" (Jn. 20:17a). Mary can no longer cling to an earthly presence, or to any other object of her old desire. From now on she is liberated from the earth. Her contemplative practice of withdrawal, of poverty of spirit, of being nothing in the church now renders her free for another task wholly unforeseen. From her place in the heavens with the risen Christ, where he has called her even as she lives in this world, in the space of suspended animation that is certainly not of here, but not yet fully of there, she announces the full import of the resurrection. Jesus continues, "But go to my brothers and say to them, 'I am ascending to my Father and your Father, to my God and your God'" (Jn. 20:17b).

To the contemplatives of a pure order, and in imitation of Mary Magdalene, goes the mission to announce the resurrection by the radical nature of their lives. This is their place in the church, to do nothing else than to proclaim the new life in Christ, which begins here but is agonizingly unfulfilled until it is consummated there. The true contemplatives hold up the sagging end of the tent of the Pilgrim People of God where the heavenly realm is announced and is palpably, if partially, realized even in this world. Their mission is to stand tall and hold up what is usually forgotten or neglected in the rush of seemingly more urgent business. In their empty end of the church, they are misunderstood, vilified or simply ignored. So it has always been with those whose burden is to carry the prophetic Word of God to those who don't want to hear it. Just touch the powdered fashion of the world and its attitudes, even in the church, which cling so closely to the familiar and the fleshly, and you will find yourself stung with vituperative slang, concocted from the swiftest conclusions drawn from furious premises. The contemplatives must remain true to their calling, or they become salt that is no longer tasteful. They must learn to shun the agents of compromise and mitigation that would sully the purity of love and smirch the garment of their tryst. They must learn to face the onslaught of outright rejection, or neglect, and the lack of generosity in a faithless age.

"For your love is better than life, my lips will speak your praise. So I will bless you all my life, in your name I will lift up my hands" (Ps. 62[63]:4-5). How is the desire of contemplatives surrendered to the Holy Spirit so that it holds heaven and earth together? How is it turned from every shadow of the fleshly order so as to join the movement of the blessed back to the Father through Christ in the Spirit? The answer lies in the movement of the same Spirit to elicit in us the love of Christ to the point where all is reduced to it. St. Paul puts it eloquently:

> *For I am convinced that neither death, nor life, nor angels, nor rulers, nor things present, nor things to come, nor powers, nor height, nor depth, nor anything else in all creation, will be able to separate us from the love of God in Christ Jesus our Lord* (Rom. 8:38-9).

The contemplative life consists in the withdrawal from all things, as much as possible, that do not flow from the exercise of unceasing prayer. One's entire life becomes centered around prayer and its variants. From the chanting of the choral office, to *Lectio Divina*, to meditation, to simple prayer formulas at work (and the less technically demanding the work the better for prayer concentration), to the observance of silence and recollected demeanor, the monk is supported and surrounded with prayer. Any other activity in which the monk may engage must flow out of this first and basic surrender to Christ in prayer. Study in the library should be in function of a more fervent *Lectio Divina*. Artistic activity may perhaps train the heart and mind in the ways of discipline and diligence. Recreational walks and even runs should bolster the love of God in creation and support a healthy bodily life. But everything always comes back to the one thing necessary, the love of Christ, to which nothing is to be preferred (see RSB 4:21; 72:11).

For monks and nuns, the long journey to this preferment of Christ begins when one is called to the monastery and adopts the structures of prayer. The monastic observance needs to be flexible enough so that newcomers can stretch their passions in the throes of surrender, one by one. This offering often takes years, much patience and great determination. Many leave off the struggle and return to the world where they often reapply fruitfully what they learned in the monastery. But for those who remain on the way, and who desire to keep faithful to the calling, there remains the slow and inevitable death to each of their loves. At first, according to the Rule, one experiences the good success of the monastic order and culture which restores life and breath to the heart and the soul, as well as the body, after a long experience of the mindless pace and violence of our worldly culture (see RSB Prol. 29-31). But after the first blush of success, one enters the long years of sacrifice and struggle to keep our minds in harmony with our voices and our actions in tune with the Gospel.

Personal and individual ambition seek to dominate the monk even in the midst of the monastic culture. One does not see, after a while, how one tends gradually to twist everything around to the satisfaction of one's own will. The monastery frequently becomes a hell where the power of the fittest seems to hold sway. The juniors never seem to be listened to by the seniors. The seniors have no wish to change anything they have become accustomed to. In such a situation, and these are many, the world enters the cloister before any open break with the Rule. In our time, the world is invited openly into the monastery in the form of media technology, which has become so privatized as to militate against the very fabric of community life. Concurrent with these developments goes the impossibility of any more physical withdrawal. The planet has become too small. Wilderness has receded. The simplicity of markets where monastic goods could be sold for necessary goods at the edge of society has disappeared. The automobile has reduced distances. Retreat houses lie within an airplane flight. The desert—the cloister, the sacred space so beloved by the desert monks and nuns, the Cistercians, and so many other groups—has become a shadow of itself. Yet there remains the call of the Spirit to come apart and proclaim the resurrection.

The love of Christ requires new and creative responses to this crisis in contemplative monastic desire. Otherwise, we risk losing our place in the church. And the church has never had greater need of the contemplative monastic way. Two insights, coming from the tradition itself, can swell the desire for God and attract the Holy Spirit to the monastic ecclesia. They are enormously unpopular in our culture today, even to the point of being considered taboo, that is, the detritus from the misdirected insights of a former time. Yet these two concepts may hold the key to the renewal of contemplative monastic life.

"We (Philip) have found him about whom Moses in the law and also the prophets wrote, Jesus son of Joseph from Nazareth.' Nathanael said to him, 'Can anything good come out of Nazareth?'" (Jn. 1:45-46). Let St. Gregory the Great introduce the first of these concepts when he wrote at the beginning of his life of St. Benedict that the holy man, turning aside from formal studies, preferred the habit of holy conversation. He withdrew to the desert "knowingly not knowing, and wisely untaught."[1] By this comment St. Gregory wishes us to understand that the monk does not make learning the mark of his love of Christ. He does not exercise his gifts of writing, teaching, exposition or any other scholarly activity in a way that gives him an identity or career in the monastery.

In fact, any gift which the monk possesses by the grace of God, he must be willing to drop, just as Simon and Andrew dropped their nets, in order to follow Christ. The world constantly tempts the monk, even in the depths of his heart, to pursue glory in what he excels. The monk called to contemplative prayer often finds that his gifts, and how he thinks about them and how he is appreciated for them, undergo a kind of unlearning and undoing. He is more free now for the holy conversation St. Gregory mentions. I am not talking here of a ruthless excising of the good gifts God has given a monk. With the proper discernment, many gifts can be cultivated fruitfully and profitably in a healthy monastic culture. Indeed, monasteries have contributed liberally to the culture of Christendom in both East and West. But I am pointing out that the call to contemplative prayer softens a monk, especially a talented, sophisticated one, so that he feels himself impoverished, lacking sheen, no longer with his peers in any specialty. The dying to sophistication, to standards the world has canonized, to a reputation one had once enjoyed is all part of a further call into a purer love. The sacrifice of gifts

---

[1] Gregorius Magnus, *Dialogii*, Liber Secundus, "De vita et miraculi venerabilis Benedicti Abbatis," SC 260 (Les Éditions du Cerf, 1979), p. 126 (my own translation). In English, *Life and Miracles of St. Benedict* (Liturgical Press, no date), p. 2.

for the sake of God entails great hardship in the heart of a monk. But if he can write, sing, play, build, run, carve, paint, count, organize, or whatever else he may do, all for the glory of God, with no audience, no reward, no building of a reputation, if he can do all the above, seemingly in a complete vacuum, then he is in real possession of his gift. It goes with him into his eternity with God. All else is vanity.

Outsiders, and even insiders, indulge in labeling monks as good at this or that, instead of honoring the anonymity which should clothe their monastic existence. If the monk has an educational pedigree, or a social one, he should endeavor to hide it so as to join the sameness of the monastic culture, wherein lies the richness of the manifold wisdom of Christ. The monk is invited to become not so sophisticated, with no accomplishments or identities except the one given him by his habit. This is not a recommendation to an anti-intellectual stance or a glorification of tasteless culture. But it is to say that the discernment of all things, especially how one spends one's time and how one gossips about oneself and postures over against the others in the community, is to be rigorous. In this age of the preening of the best, the competition for titles, the contests for prizes, the monk called to a pure love must learn to eschew all of these things. He must be willing to absorb the dismissal of those who are too willing to look down on him with pity. Can he imitate Jesus of Nazareth, who willingly endured the scorn of Nathanael and of numerous Pharisees, who had predetermined that his pedigree, apparently forlorn of the Temple, was not worthy of them? Let Gregory the Great and his teaching on the want of sophistication be our guide.

"For while we were still weak, at the right time Christ died for the ungodly" (Rom. 5:6). The second concept that lifts the desire for God to a burning fire is sacrifice. Our culture, so intent on the self-development of the individual, so recklessly crazy over the dominance of the person over others (and we never seem to worry about the others), so careful to hold open all options in case a better opportunity should arise (and we define "better" as more self-glorifying), grows silent in the face of sacrifice. Generosity, yes. Magnanimity, of course. But dying for the sake of another? It makes no sense to us. Perhaps the most difficult concept in the

Christ event, that Christ should die on the cross as a sacrifice for our redemption, smacks too much of a God who makes demands, and requires satisfactions, and cares nothing about the suffering of the poor and the dominated. A willing death for a cause, an artistic one, a political one, or the risk of death for a medical cause, we can understand and even approve of. But a death for God, a voluntary snuffing out of life's possibilities or the conscious strangling of gifts, these we cannot tolerate. We object that life and all its splendiferous development is God's gift and that we should develop it for the sake of his glory. We forget about the call of the love of God, which also snuffed out his Christ in a righteous deed for us. We cannot fathom his reasons for righting by the cross of his Son, the wrong we have done his love. We cannot fully understand his longing to re-establish his intimacy with us. He alone knows the price of love. We call foolish the way of the cross, since with death there is no more chance to praise the Lord on this earth. In the church, we know with what great care the martyrs discerned the call to death, how they postponed it, in many cases, until they were sure that the call was from God, who loves life and wills the joy of his creatures. Yet the concept of sacrifice endures, and is proclaimed at every Eucharist and on every cross. It touches a great truth to which our culture has turned a deaf ear and a blind eye. As often as we celebrate the Eucharist, we fade out the unpleasantness of the cross, as we do so much else of life, and concentrate on those aspects of the Mass that comfort us and affirm us in our lukewarmness. The Scriptures will not be gainsaid. The Gospel teaching stands firm: that if you want to live, you must die (see Mt. 10:39). And if you want to live with Christ, you must be willing to enter completely into your baptismal grace that joins you to his death so that you might rise with him to new life. The monk, to the extent that he can accept the call to sacrifice his life in the monastery, emblazes on the church the sacrifice of Christ for all to see. He glorifies it in his own sacrifice. He joins Christ's own redeeming death and glorification which is celebrated unceasingly in the heavenly liturgy.

Talk of sacrifice, however, is easy. It drips effortlessly from the mouth. Sacrifice is a slow, halting process which the monk endures like a cripple dragging a leg or a shattered foot. To enlighten this painful approach to the altar of sacrifice, I turn to Christ. Did not Jesus take to himself these verses of Psalm 21[22] which he invoked while hanging on the cross (Mt. 27:26)?

> *But I am a worm and no man,*
> *the butt of men, laughing-stock of the people.*
> *All who see me deride me.*
> *They curl their lips, they toss their heads* (Ps. 21[22]:7-8).

Did he not endure the taunts of his accusers that his life of service to others was useless? What were his thoughts when, on the cross, he had become a dead tree, life-giving to no one and dying to himself with nothing to show for it? His disciples had fled. His intimates had crumbled in fear at his arrest, and his hand-picked leader, chosen on a day of brilliant, resplendent confession, was now hiding somewhere like a dog, weeping bitterly. The world of Jesus—his purpose, preaching and ministry—was ending in the ashes of his own burnt offering. He was tasting down to the bitterness of the gall, the price of sacrifice.

The great trial of Jesus (is it any surprise?) may also be the trial of the monk who stands with him at the foot of the cross. Consider a man or woman in their fifties after having been two or three decades in the monastery. What are the feelings when the all too short burst of youthful enthusiasm is over? Having followed his star for many years in happy faith, the monk looks around him and notices that everybody else has settled down from their youth. They have married, given children to society, secured, perhaps, their name, had the joy of seeing in a young-ster's eyes their own hopes for life. The monk is aware that the bustle of a busy room, with his gifts coming and going through its doors, is growing quieter as the doors close, imperceptibly, he knows not how, one by one. The monk feels caught. He thinks he hears the taunts somewhere in the air around him. "Look at what you have done to yourself. You have nothing. You have spent your energies uselessly among vapid and unappreciative people. They care nothing for you. You could have known love and togetherness. You could have enjoyed at least a moderate success. You could now be counting grandchildren. Yet, you have nothing to show for your sacrifice. As you get older, all you will have is regret."

Another voice whirls around in the air above the middle-aged monk or nun. "You have wasted your life and wasted your gifts. Who told you that God accepts burnt offerings? Did the Teacher not say that one should develop one's talents so as to make profit for the Master? You have squandered yours. You have buried the little that you have. What do you think awaits you at the end? You will come before him with nothing and you will be cast out."

Real sacrifice of one's life in a contemplative monastery includes, with no doubt, these thoughts and temptations, replete with derisions and insults. No sacrifice is complete, no offering consummated without the lingering smell of the last burning ash of the heap once piled high. Unless one tastes this ashen nothingness, one cannot know completely the Savior. One cannot be joined to him. Only from our cross can we get to his. Only in the darkest faith through a wasted life filled with thoughts of what could have been can one wait for an arresting compassionate dawn.

Monks and nuns of our Order in Europe and North America know the same elements of sacrifice but with new twists and more dire outcomes. Many of us see our sacrifice as unfruitful even in the community which was flourishing when we entered but today is obviously dying. We wonder what the taunts mean coming to us from the church: passé, out of step, silly, too rigorous, too little structure, lax and unfaithful to their tradition, and so many more. We reason that the economic prosperity of our time has strangled the thought of heaven, untied the bonds of final commitment, and redirected the generosity of youth either to models of the past or to two or three years of volunteer work where outcomes and successes are visible. We acknowledge that our renewal has rendered us knowing but unknowing, wise but untaught, and naïve in our silence. We simply have no answer to the questions posed us. Yet one thing we know. The voice of the wild Spirit is going unheeded in the church. It still blows warm but cools as it hits rigid or stony hearts. Yet we must believe that the Spirit will raise, and is raising, up groups in the church where the free abandon of the love of God in the heart of a monk will be offered in sacrifice. For us, who must stand by and watch the church move on, our sacrifice is clothed with the bands of sorrow that engulfed Mary and Martha at the tomb. Jesus weeps with us. We await the glory of God.

**"Jesus said to her (Martha) 'Did I not tell you that if you be-
lieved, you would see the glory of God?' So they took away the
stone" (Jn. 11:40-41).** Sacrifice and the want of sophistication lift
the monk's prayer beyond that of his own strength. By his embrace of these, he approaches the borderline of his own efforts.
At this point in his spiritual life, the Spirit removes the foundations of his own monastic way so that even the little monastic
identity he possessed, in a kind of spiritual sophistication, falls
to the ground. The monk is made to see that of himself he is
nothing, not even a monk. There is nothing left for him to do but
call upon God in his nakedness and emptiness. At this point, too,
the Spirit accepts his offering of sacrifice, scoops up the precious
contents of his life, and distributes them to those elsewhere in
the church who may need them. The offering of the monk is now
complete. There is no turning back to reclaim what once was his
own. There is no moving forward, since there is no fuel in his
being to propel him. He is alone and poured out. But what can
be stated is that the monk's desire is no longer tainted with this
world's passions. He is quieted. Even more importantly, his
prayer to Jesus as a kind of mantra against his proclivities,
thoughts and prejudices ceases. The Spirit reduces the monk to
this level of abasing self-knowledge in order to grant a new and
unsuspected grace. Like Lazarus in the tomb, he is called out of
death and confinement and lets the Spirit unbind him and let
him go free. He tenderly lifts the broken monk to a new level
which the ancients described as a kind of resurrection, even in
the here and now. Jesus proclaims: *I am the resurrection and the
life. Those who believe in me, even though they die, will live, and everyone who lives and believes in me will never die* (Jn. 11:25b-26). In this
first resurrection, the monk's self-purification is at an end. His
dependence on prayer as a technique and a payment against the
debt of sin, and a bribe to God to stay in the monastery, gets
swallowed up by a constant interior reassurance that his journey
is now out of his hands and in the power of the Holy Spirit. The
monk can no longer enjoy the things he used to enjoy nor employ
them according to his own custom. Everything earthly is new,
but in shadow, softened, moderated, and dimmed. His expectation changes from the next project, and the next stimulation, to
a new desire for the kingdom of heaven and its peace. He has

been struck, as Jacob was, and can no longer walk in the health of this world. He is content and even honored to be that thing he once counted as so dreadful, a eunuch for the sake of the kingdom of heaven (see Mt. 19:12). The monk's prayer is now able to penetrate the silences that before it feared. The emptiness of time and space beckons him. The passing moments order a new stillness. The suffering of all things as they come to be and pass away is blessed by him and participated in by his own patience. The love of the enemy and the other, upheld in the Gospel, while never easy, is possible not by his doing but by the Holy Spirit. Who can describe this freedom? Who can narrate this experience? What language can convey it? What tongue can celebrate it? What poem can contain it?

"And we speak of these things in words not taught by human wisdom but taught by the Spirit, interpreting spiritual things to those who are spiritual. Those who are unspiritual do not receive the gifts of God's Spirit, for they are foolishness to them, and they are unable to understand them because they are spiritually discerned" (1 Cor. 2:13-14). Let me remind the reader that anyone who is gifted with this transformation sinks back into the community unsung and unknown. These gifts are not to be trumpeted, nor can they be discerned by the unspiritual. There is no celebration of sanctity, nor are there attempts at biographies, tales, and edifying stories for the faithful. The hiddenness of the transformed is absolute and presided over by the Holy Spirit. Yet the monk is content to be a channel of grace for others and to be generative in the church.

Only after the Spirit has taken up the life of the monk can chaste celibacy be discussed with any meaning. Chaste celibacy can be called the transformation of desire. The possibilities for being with another, for working out one's salvation with another, are closed off intentionally but not without a call from God and the grace to maintain it. The call to marriage and sexual reproduction comes from God himself and is honored by all cultures. But the call to celibacy presupposes an arduous road that never ends in bodily life. The religious celibate is asked nothing less than to transfer his/her desire into an unseen form. That transfer of desire requires a strong and well-guarded structure to keep desire authentic without deadening it by other pursuits not religious. So the stuff of monastic observance, eventually enlivened by the Holy Spirit, becomes the very anatomy of desire for the kingdom of heaven.

Desire for God contains within itself the yearning for sharing and participating with others along the spiritual journey. It finds a generative wish in every relationship, the like of which is far more lasting and cogent even than the urge to have children or grandchildren. It simply goes with the landscape of desire. Any spiritual person, according to the terms laid out above, is automatically generative in the Holy Spirit. One may not see the results of one's generative desire, because the lack of tangible results goes hand in hand with the hiddenness of the Spirit. Still, one may see the stirrings of spiritual birth in the brothers or sisters one lives with. New, authentic and magnanimous life always flows from genuinely spiritual persons, simply because the kingdom of God is breaking forth in their lives.

What can be said for generative life flowing from the heart of the believer to others in a local community can be confidently asserted for the whole church as well. How can this be? How can one know this, and trust it, and find the energy and power in a radically ascetic life to live it? The answer lies in the grace of baptism itself. In baptism we drink of the waters of Christ. But the grace of our baptism does not end with consumption but, rather, with distribution. All are baptized in the same water from the mystic Jordan of the church's font made holy by Christ's baptism. All drink of the Spirit of Christ. All are connected in one body by that unifying stream. Those who sink down deeply into the waters of Christ's death and regeneration also rise up out of the waters rich in his Spirit. The Spirit distributes the gifts of God to the People of God. He makes the church fruitful at its very depth where all the world is offered holiness, and where the church is continually born and structured with no national boundaries, no barriers of language, no confines of time or space. As Jesus himself puts it:

> *(On the last day of the festival, the great day, while Jesus was standing there, he cried out), "Let anyone who is thirsty come to me, and let the one who believes in me drink. As the scripture has*

said, 'Out of the believer's heart shall flow rivers of living water.'"
Now he said this about the Spirit, which believers in him were to
receive; for as yet there was no Spirit, because Jesus was not yet
glorified (Jn. 7:37-39).

All over the world, the Spirit calls people to this transformation of becoming life-giving beings for others. Though many and
divided, the spiritual are yet one, bridging in the Spirit the
diversity of the world's nations and cultures. A movement away
in one corner of the church, at first hidden, insignificant, and of
no consequence, may grow like the mustard seed to be the greatest of all shrubs in the church and be a source of evangelization
and conversion for many of our brothers and sisters. The Spirit
also keeps the church in balance to opt always for the unseen
which lies hidden behind the passing things of this world. These
considerations, however, are mere fancy compared to the Spirit's
most important work—that of pulling together in the church all
of the faithful who can stand before the Son of Man into a new
unity of movement back to the Father through Christ.

The rules of God's game are that we cannot see this movement or discern it with fleshly eyes. Yet our faith tells us that this
call and this movement have already started and are proceeding
with great haste toward the culmination of all things. Joining,
celebrating and proclaiming with their lives the forward movement in the Spirit, through Christ, back to the Father is the
principal work of the monastic contemplatives. This is the final
content of the desire of monks and nuns. Desire is now seen to
be not so much theirs but actually the desire of the Holy Spirit,
the Spirit of Christ, for God the Father. As monumental as desire
can seem in our experience, as raging hot as its flames may
threaten, it pales in comparison with this new and unspeakable
desire which we now experience. We are privileged to taste something of the desire within God himself. Incredibly, God's desire
becomes our desire also, just as God's divinity is shared with us
in Christ. The participation in this divinity is more than talk. The
Holy Spirit fulfills our baptismal grace by joining us to Christ,
so that we become spiritual even in this world. Then we know
Christ not in the way we once knew him. For, to the extent that
we have been made spiritual, we are in him, and he in us. We are

no longer separate, and, therefore, our prayer to him changes. How can we pray to ourselves? The person we now know (dimly) is his Spirit who begins in us the return journey to God the Father. This is the reason Christ came and the reason he was glorified, so that the human person may join him in the movement of the Spirit back to the Father.

> *Likewise the Spirit helps us in our weakness; for we do not know how to pray as we ought, but that very Spirit intercedes with sighs too deep for words. And God, who searches the heart, knows what is the mind of the Spirit, because the Spirit intercedes for the saints according to the will of God* (Rom. 8:26-27).

This is perhaps the best way of describing the contemplative life in the church. Not a prayer style, not a mystic approach to life, but, rather, the enjoyment of the gift of divine life tasted as the Spirit's desire for God, and the passionate, even ecstatic, groaning and desirous movement of the Spirit through Christ, back to the Father.

With our place in the church stated in this way, we are not so much "extras" off the stage of reality but "principals," along with all the rest of the People of God called to holiness. Our place in the church simply must go recognized at the risk of its great diminishment.

"Let my prayer arise before you like incense, the raising of my hands like an evening oblation" (Ps. 140[141]:2). The prayer of the People of God is fired by their desire for God. How many are those desires! They range from one's personal needs, one's fear of God for salvation, one's care for loved ones, to love of God for his own sake, to love of God even more than one's life, and, finally, to the love of the will of God in perfect freedom. This enormous scale of desire illumines the prayer of monastic contemplatives. Using the same prayer of the church, for example, the Opus Dei, in monastic parlance, or the "Liturgy of the Hours" in the language of the universal church, the monastic contemplatives pour into it a content that only the Spirit can give, for only the Spirit could so enrich it. As I complete this essay on desire, I turn to the one prayer in the *Opus Dei* known to all, the "Our

Father," taught by Jesus himself to his disciples and included in every office prayed in the church. The monastic contemplatives pray this prayer with the spiritual desire which comes from God alone. They pray in the evening of this world, where we ask Christ to stay with us for the last leg of the journey. Monastic contemplatives see the world as passing away, and the new world of God's kingdom always breaking out in celebration when one sinner repents. They pray the Lord's Prayer with eyes and ears enlightened to the truth of all things. Yet it is the same prayer prayed throughout the church. This unity of prayer, yet the very diversity of its content, is how best to understand the universal call to holiness. All are called to it. All are asked to live it to its fulfillment. The monastic contemplatives light up the way of the one same holiness even to its consummation in the fulfillment of the Scriptures at the end of the world.

"Our Father in heaven . . ." (Mt. 6:9b). So much of our prayer is personal, that, at first glance the title "Our Father" may not fit well on our lips. Notice in conversation how often in the presence of siblings from the same parents a son or daughter calls the mother or father, "my mother or father." The relationship between the two is unique and insisted upon, even in the presence of brothers and sisters. The analogy can be employed all across the human spectrum in every activity. That which enjoins my activity becomes my possession, and I proclaim it as such, even when I know that others have participated and, perhaps, even authored the project. The truth of my own participation blots out the truth of the rights of the others. I convince myself of my rights over an entity and believe in my own half lie. I maintain my territory all the more fiercely as I continue to believe my own sovereignty. Jesus' invocation at the beginning of the Lord's Prayer invites his followers to go beyond the self into the communion of saints, that is, the church, where one would not, even cannot, pray outside of it. The sacrifice of self, in imitation of Christ, once consummated by the Holy Spirit, is forever. The "Our Father" begins with a challenge for those on this side of transformation, and for those on the other side, it is the truth.

"Father" raises all sorts of issues in our time, none of them particularly cogent for our purposes here. First of all, "Father" is the name of God revealed to us by Jesus. Its likeness with what we know of fatherhood in our culture is as limp as our love. "What shall I do with you, O Ephraim? What shall I do with you, O Judah? Your love is like a morning cloud, like the dew that goes away early" (Hos. 6:4). The Father whom Jesus names sends out his Word by the power of his Holy Spirit. That same Spirit causes the Word to become flesh, to live and die for us. The Christ, in his turn, breathes forth the Spirit into the whole world to raise up his memory in the church. The missions of the Son and the Holy Spirit, which we know about in the Scriptures, only hint at the mystery of relationships in the Godhead: Father, Son, and Holy Spirit. Gender, as we define it, is not appropriate here. Though we can feel the now-masculine, now-feminine qualities of the divine action in the economy of salvation, we cannot label them as we label ourselves. Even our own gender identity suffers the loss of all temporal things as we become life-giving spirits in the kingdom of heaven. Bodily, to be sure, we are no longer needful of a complementary partner, since our fulfillment is God, and our participation in God's generativity lies in the mystery of the Trinitarian relationships. The best we can say is that our bodily presence, joined to Christ's glorious body, now enjoys the cosmic dance of ultimate fertility and ecstatic generosity. The whole of the dynamic life of the saving economy in the Father's missions of the Son and the Holy Spirit is forever. It does not cease, and though it has touched space and time, it always desires to transform them in spirit and in truth. Our language will always be inadequate to this mystery. The Scriptures reveal to us the name of "Father" and do not flinch from the full meaning of that term in the salvation economy of Father, Son, and Holy Spirit. In the full identity of the name taught to us by Christ, we pray, "Our Father."

". . . in heaven" (Mt. 6:9c). Heaven is hidden from those who lack goodness in their lives and live without faith in God and the unseen. Even for believers the concept remains just that, an idea whose truth hangs on the balance of life after death. Heaven begins with Jesus' promise of eternal life. The criminal, crucified with Jesus said to him, "Jesus, remember me when you shall come into your kingdom." Jesus replied, "Truly, I tell you, today you will be with me in Paradise" (Lk. 23:39-43). Heaven is about a relationship with God through Jesus Christ in the Holy Spirit. The language of rewards after death, of punishments after death, of living now in suffering so that we can live there in happiness is one very effective way of getting across the truth of the matter to an unbelieving or forgetful populace. In fact, it is Jesus' own method.

> *Blessed are you when people revile you and persecute you and utter all kinds of evil against you falsely on my account. Rejoice and be glad, for your reward is great in heaven, for in the same way they persecuted the prophets who were before you* (Mt. 5:12).

And,

> *Beware of practicing your piety before others in order to be seen by them; for then you have no reward from your Father in heaven* (Mt. 6:1).

In his teaching, Jesus reveals a loving and merciful God when faith is found, and when faith has grown cold, an all-consuming and uncompromising face of God. Having encountered the faith of the Roman centurion, Jesus exclaims in amazement, "Truly I tell you, in no one in Israel have I found such faith. I tell you, many will come from east and west and will eat with Abraham and Isaac and Jacob in the kingdom of heaven, while the heirs of the kingdom will be thrown into the outer darkness, where there will be weeping and gnashing of teeth" (Mt. 8:10b-13).

An even more acute delineation of the necessity of faith in order to understand heaven is given by Jesus to the Pharisees in his story of the rich man and Lazarus (see Lk. 16:19-31). The rich man lived in insouciance of the suffering around him, especially in the person of the poor man Lazarus, who lay at the rich man's gate and would have been content to eat what fell from the rich man's table. The rich man exhibits no love of goodness or generosity while he lived in this world. He was unmoved at the sight of the poor around him. He ignored God's constant plea to have pity on the hungry and the prisoner, even though probably the rich man's ancestors, too, were once poor, in prison and subjugated. In the next life, there is no place in God for the rich man. Not having known God here, he cannot possibly know him there. Heaven, that is, a relationship with God, begins here, for it is here that his Spirit prepared the way for Christ to come and make into heaven's threshold the whole of this creation. God's truth begins here. It does not wait for some abstract judgment in the afterlife. Judgment is now and always, for it lies in the secret moves of the heart for or against God. The rich man tries to bargain with God to send Lazarus to his brothers who also live in forgetfulness of God. But God remains firm in the truth of this creation and in the power of his Word. What is done here, even in this passing sphere, is forever. No signs from above, no magic shows, no messengers from beyond can break through the hardness of unbelief, once it is cemented by greediness and selfishness. These are the very opposite of God (see Lk. 16:31). Only the power of God's Word in the Scriptures can melt the iron heart and convince the skeptic mind of the truth of God's mercy. Heaven's secrets lie in the here and now. Death, once Christ has conquered death and opened up the gates of heaven, is really no barrier against heaven. Heaven is open to us in faith and the actions that flow from faith. The monastic contemplatives take St. Paul at his word when he says,

> But our citizenship is in heaven, and it is from there that we are expecting a Savior, the Lord Jesus Christ. He will transform the body of our humiliation that it may be conformed to the body of his glory, by the power that also enables him to make all things subject to himself (Phil. 3:20-21).

For them, heaven is now, and the resurrection begins to unfold its glories of the new person even in this temporal existence. In the power of the Holy Spirit, the judgment is already passed because "the ruler of this world has been condemned" (Jn. 16:11). The trial of the passage may still await us, but the power of the evil one has been overcome in us. While we are in the Spirit, we already live between heaven and earth in a relationship that provides for us a glimpse of the glory of the children of God. Those who engage in empty debates about the existence of an afterlife argue so outside of the realm of faith. Faith alone allows the belief in heaven and fosters the love of God that proves it.

". . . hallowed be your name" (Mt. 6:9c). We move from the prayer of invocation, to an evocation of praise. We cannot praise God with anything like the heavenly glory. Yet his glory is to create us and redeem us in the blood of his Son. God waits for our response. The largest part of the mystery of the human person is the ability to lift up our faces, our hearts, the whole of our being to God in praise. In this ecstatic movement, we go out of ourselves, become more than ourselves, and touch God in the spiritual kiss of recognition, love, and gratitude. From the sacrifices of the Hebrew patriarchs, the prayers of the Psalmist, and the signs and the oracles of the prophets, Israel confirmed itself as the People of God when it gave itself over to praise. The new Israel of God, the Christian church, praises God in a way more ecstatic and worthy of the grandeur and splendor of God. Joined to Christ, we enter his own prayer of praise:

> *Father, the hour has come; glorify your Son so that the Son may glorify you, since you have given him authority over all people, to give eternal life to all whom you have given him* (Jn. 17:1b-2).

We are caught up in God's own ecstatic movement out of himself in the mission of the Son, through the power of the Holy Spirit. In Christ, God is glorified. In the Spirit, through Christ, we also glorify God at last in a way that matches the fulfillment of our calling to be children of God. For those who enjoy the gift of the Spirit in contemplation, every celebration of the Eucharist, indeed, every celebration of the Liturgy of the Hours, participates in the ceaseless heavenly praise. As we worship in the Eucharist, and as we pray in the office, we are invited to hear and see with the eyes of faith the splendor of the heavenly liturgy:

> *Then I looked, and I heard the voice of many angels surrounding the throne and the living creatures and the elders; they numbered thousands of thousands, singing with full voice. "Worthy is the Lamb that was slaughtered to receive power and wealth and wisdom and might and honor and blessing!" Then I heard every*

*creature in heaven and on earth and under the earth and in the
sea, and all that is in them, singing, "To the one seated on the
throne and to the Lamb be blessing and honor and glory and might
forever and ever!"* (Rev. 5:11-14a).

The monastic contemplatives keep alive in the church the
horizon of the heavenly praise that begins in the simplest, poor-
est, and purest hearts, even if they be in the humblest circumstances, and extends all the way to the great gathering of the
whole human community in the church here on earth, with the
spiritual community of the angels and of those who have gone
before us marked with the sign of faith, as they are joined to the
glory of God in heaven.

"Your kingdom come" (Mt. 6:10a). For most in the church, this
part of the prayer aims at the end of time, when God's kingdom
will be entirely revealed in Christ when he comes in all of his
glory. Jesus' teaching and parables portray another, more proxi-
mate reality than only the end of time. In the Gospel of Matthew,
after his baptism, that is, his commission by the Father in the
Spirit to begin his public ministry, and after his preparatory so-
journ in the desert, Jesus began to proclaim, "Repent, for the
kingdom of heaven has come near" (Mt. 4:17). Indeed, God has
come near to his People in Jesus, in the whole of the movement
from his Baptism in the Jordan, to his sending of the Spirit after
his death and resurrection. Wherever the poor have the Gospel
preached to them, wherever the release of captives is proclaimed,
the recovery of sight to the blind is bestowed, and all the other
signs that the Holy One of God has appeared, according to the
Scriptures, there, Jesus assures us, the kingdom of God is at hand
(see Lk. 4:16-19). The parables about the kingdom delineate a
dynamic reality that is compared to the unpredictable moves of
the nature around us, as well as our own human nature, especially the movements of the heart. The kingdom is like a mustard
seed, the smallest of seeds, that grows into a lofty tree boasting
of birds in its branches. The kingdom is like yeast in the dough
that leavens the entire loaf. The kingdom is like a man who finds
a treasure in a field and sacrifices all that he has to buy the field
with the treasure in it. The kingdom grows mysteriously, according to the whim of the Spirit, and not according to any human

calculation. It attracts the human person who responds with extraordinary enthusiasm. The authority of Jesus, his righteousness before the religious leaders of Israel, his signs and miracles, all point to the active presence of the Spirit of God among his People. And where God is, there the kingdom is present. Not in some future realm after this world, but right within this world the kingdom begins to come.

In its sacramental theology, the church teaches that Jesus' signs, miracles, and teaching continue as the church celebrates the sacraments. By the sending of his Spirit, Christ guarantees his presence among us in a way that grows exponentially according to the dynamics of faith. Inspired preaching, as in the case of St. Paul, leads to more adherents to the faith. More and more people celebrate the sacraments, and the kingdom of heaven takes on a life of its own even in the here and now. Perhaps this is the best definition of the church, the kingdom of heaven come to the earth. Mysterious and hidden, this kingdom will not be subject to numbers counting, political embrace, or the preferment of one group over another. The challenge of the church lies in its willingness to be the kingdom of heaven on earth. When it moors itself to human traditions, allies itself with earthly forces, enters into the thickets of party spirit and ideological divisions, it loses its frontal ability to be the sign of the kingdom of heaven. It may at times appear as a countersign to the Gospel. Yet the mystery of the church remains. It cannot be reduced to a temporal reality, subject to human influence and maneuver. Even those who would criticize the church for its infidelities must bow to the authentic prophets sent to it by the Holy Spirit. Otherwise, our place is to fall silent before the mystery and discern in faith where the kingdom is most authentic in the church. Wherever we are in the church, we can begin to move in our restricted circle according to the radical teaching of the Gospel. In unsung and unnoticed holy corners of the church, it is most itself.

Monastic contemplatives, and those with whom they join hands in the transformation of Christ, pray in the purest way for God's kingdom to come. In them, there is no barrier against the free moves of faith. No resistance to God's ways can be identified in their hearts. In their lives they embody the kingdom and in their prayer of desire for the kingdom, they effectively bridge the chasm between the temporal here and the eternal there. As the kingdom works in their lives, it knows less and less restrictions of space or time, and knows more and more the freedom of the children of God. The body itself becomes a temple of the Holy Spirit, in word and in deed. How effective is the mercy of God come into the world through the hearts of those who pray for the kingdom? How powerful is their ceaseless prayer, day and night, for the staving off of the violent and the greedy? How responsible are these holy ones for the prevention of a final slaughter of fundamentalism and genocide? Only when the kingdom is fully revealed will the world know how it was saved by those whose whole desire was to pray.

"Your will be done, on earth as it is in heaven" (Mt. 6:10bc). The spiritual journey begins out of the cyclic ruins of our culture when the faithful hearken in their hearts to the will of God. The cliché, to do the will of God, is drained of its ephemeral wordiness, when the person is confronted with the stubbornness of God in the face of our own stubbornness. Jacob had to be wrestled to the point of injury. David had to endure betrayal by his own offspring in order to come to repentance. Elijah had to be coaxed out of his cave and his mood so as to anoint Elisha to succeed him. Jesus' disciples encounter the fierceness of the demons who, at their command, refuse to come out of the possessed. Yet the demons always submit to the will of God in Jesus. Shall we not attribute the great love which Mary Magdalene showed Jesus to her cleansing from seven demons? Is this an Hebraic number meaning that she was totally in the power of the evil one? Jesus cast out of her the corrupting spirits so that she returned his favor with much love. St. Paul, on the road to Damascus, fell to the ground with God's great light all around him. This shattering experience turned him from a persecutor of the church to its fiercest liberator. In all three accounts of this conversion, we always hear similar words to St. Paul: "You will be told what you are to do" (Acts 9:6; 22:10; 26:16-18). Another account by St. Paul in Galatians gets us closer to the mystery of the will of God and human freedom.

> *You have heard, no doubt, of my earlier life in Judaism. I was violently persecuting the church of God and was trying to destroy it. I advanced in Judaism beyond many among my people of the same*

age, for I was far more zealous for the traditions of my ancestors. But when God, who had set me apart before I was born and called me through his grace, was pleased to reveal his Son to me, so that I might proclaim him among the Gentiles (Gal. 1:13-16).

Our only freedom is to do God's will. Blinded by our fear and guilt, and the cumulative lies abundant in our folk and intellectual cultures, we insist on thinking that we are on an even match with God, his will or ours. The truth is that we have only one choice for life, to love God and live and be fulfilled by the promises he has made to us in Christ. The other choice is to curse God and fall into diminishment. There is simply no neutral stance, no way to opt out of this offer of love. Those who choose to reject God live in darkness and bitterness. Love cannot be forced on anyone. It cannot be the object of a bribe. It cannot be half-hearted or lukewarm, for then it is not love. The great drama of the struggle between God and the human person is illustrated in the lives of the spiritually exalted. But for most of us, a choice is made, without the lights of God or the torments of the elements, or the appearance of angels, but, rather, in a tortured inner struggle where we learn and accept the truth of our situation before God and, gradually, submit ourselves to his will.

With most of us, God is, therefore, gentle and most patient, giving us the whole time of our lives on earth to come to a greater understanding of our situation and to accept in freedom and desire his offer of love. We cannot question God's ways with another. A conversion to him may happen at the very last moment, in the case of the criminal next to Jesus at his crucifixion. On the other hand, a long, slow process of initiation gradually convinces us of the love of God, so that we may no longer hold out against God. Each of us is embarked on a journey totally unique to ourselves. If we are set apart by God before our birth, and this is the constant tradition in the Scriptures regarding those called to special tasks in the economy of salvation, we celebrate that election in the church. But for most of us, the way of faith is bittersweet, perduring, with only occasional moments of clarity. Are we then to look jealously at others who may have received more than we? Are we to lament our apparent spiritual poverty in the face of the riches of others? Would we bother about the mystery of election, which we shall know about eventually, but which simply has no bearing on our life of faith? Or do we suppose that Jesus' death is not enough for us? Did he die for only a few? The liturgy reminds us in the words of consecration: "Take this, all of you, and drink from it: this is the cup of my blood, the blood of the new and everlasting covenant. It will be shed for you and for all so that sins may be forgiven" (Roman Liturgy: Eucharistic Prayer III). Is the salvific content of the outpoured blood of the Lord lessened in my case or made greater for someone else? Would we prefer anything but God's personal way with us? If we lament the spiritual dryness that sucks up much of our lives, would we still be willing to throw over those words of Jesus to Thomas, "Have you believed because you have seen me? Blessed are those who have not seen and yet have come to believe" (Jn. 20:29). Enough for us to hear the words which the inventive slave heard at the time of his master's return: "Well done, good and trustworthy slave; you have been trustworthy in a few things, I will put you in charge of many things; enter into the joy of your master" (Mt. 25:21b).

The contemplatives can pray, "Your will be done on earth as it is in heaven," because their desire for God has gone beyond the desire to do their own will. Their love of God has been so taken up into the movement of God's own love that they are not anxious over their salvation. They readily accept any chastisement or purification that may come to them. They can rejoice in any perceived preferment by God of others over them. Their sights are no longer on themselves but on the Lord, his ways, and his will. Gone is the protective shield that holds out against God. Overcome and transformed is the ambition that lurks deep in the heart of every human being. Empty is the human desire to assert oneself in the face of God. The only independence left in the monastic contemplative is that which clings to God and delights in a communion with him.

"Give us this day our daily bread" (Mt. 6:11). The range of the application of this prayer is extensive. For many in the world, it means just that—the plea for daily physical sustenance where famine, political actions, wars, and the unjust manipulation of the world's goods have resulted in the lack of proper nourishment for millions of God's children. The plea does not end there.

Many more struggle to make financial ends meet in a fiercely competitive job market. Single-parent families are the hardest hit. But many other families wrestle with the issues of childcare versus adequate incomes for education and entitlement of their children. Their cry for daily physical sustenance has more to do with a balanced budget than with the actual food on the table. Millions more find themselves caught in the waves of immigration that are flowing over our world at this time. Uprooted, harassed, and rejected, these people pray in a way that God the Father hears, and he will answer their cry for help.

For the rest of us who are in the stream of relative economic security, the prayer for daily bread takes on additional meanings. For many, it is simply the spiritual strength to go through another day of commitment, toleration, and self-giving. We need sustenance from God without which we feel we cannot survive the day. Our plea becomes critical to the fulfillment of our daily schedule, for we have loaded upon ourselves burdens too heavy to bear. Caught in the net of perceived injustice, in our families or in the workplace, we cover over our resentment and anger with a cloth of civility and even Gospel rectitude. Not having the spiritual development at our base to sustain us, we careen top-heavy throughout the day, ready at once to tip over in frustration and rage with the weight of our goodness.

God waits for our crash. Not ready, however, to allow him further into our stronghold of sensitivities and hurts stemming from what we think is unjust treatment, we use his own exclamatory statement as our mantra:

> *Come to me, all you that are weary and are carrying heavy burdens, and I will give you rest. Take my yoke upon you, and learn from me; for I am gentle and humble in heart, and you will find rest for your souls. For my yoke is easy, and my burden is light* (Mt. 11:28-30).

We long for that comfort from the Lord. We are content with the crumbs of consolation that may come our way from his Spirit. These keep us on the track of fidelity, even though we come frighteningly close to veering off. We feel relieved, we go on, and our house goes protected by our automatic alarms and our barking dogs. In the end nothing much changes, because we have not taken Christ's offer to heart. He says quite simply, "Come to me . . ." (Mt. 11:28a). The only way we can come is on his terms, not on ours. If we know deep down in our hearts that we would come to him with a mask of posturing, a persona that we offer to the world but that the Lord would not recognize, then we cannot come. If we consider falsely that the exterior persona is all there is to us, that underneath we remain essentially unworthy of God, we will not come. But if our desire for God excavates below our persona and finds there a being thirsting for God despite our self-knowledge, then we are ready to dismantle ourselves in humility and come to him as baldly as he asks.

We remember that, in the Gospel of Matthew, just before this comforting exclamation of our Lord, he had said,

> *I thank you, Father, Lord of heaven and earth, because you have hidden these things from the wise and the intelligent and have revealed them to infants; yes, Father, for such was your gracious will* (Mt. 11:25-26a).

Jesus invokes the image of the child as the one to whom God reveals the secrets of the kingdom, by which he means his Son, come to us in the mysterious mission of the Father's love in the enfolding mysterious cloud of the Spirit. The Father's love in the missions of both the Son and the Spirit are unspeakable and not knowable by our intelligence. But they are revealed to the one who, childlike, learns to receive everything from the hand of God. In the learned habit of love, the childlike one either never acquires the skill to put on the human fear/arrogance of our kind, or else unlearns those sophistications so as to become naïve, unsuspecting, unguarded, and spontaneous before God. In the face of all the "foes" of daily existence, the childlike person learns to have no fear because God is ever present, as if holding the hand, guarding the way, close inside the shirt. The childlike one becomes brave in that confidence. Jesus used startling images to insist on God's intimate care for us.

> *Do not fear those who kill the body but cannot kill the soul; rather fear him who can destroy both soul and body in hell. Are not two*

sparrows sold for a penny? Yet not one of them falls to the ground apart from your Father. And even the hairs of your head are all counted. So do not be afraid; you are of more value than many sparrows (Mt. 10:28-31).

The unmasking of all our sophistications, the untying of all our strings of fear by the faith in the Lord's presence, renders us awkward and even crippled in this world. We depend confidently on the Spirit to help us walk upright and to keep us steady on our feet. The Spirit brings out of our depths an innocence at once childlike but also clever and wise. The innocence comes from a pure love of the Lord, restorative, life-finding, unburdened by bribes and posturing, which frees the eyes to see the truth of what is really before us. The truly innocent person becomes fearless. The bravery and the wisdom come from the knowledge of our weakness and the learned dependence on the power of the Holy Spirit for protection from the evil one when he appears in any guise in persons and things. Walking with the Lord on the earth as if in the garden of paradise, stripped of all the clothing of shame and guilt, full of knowledge of the darkness which screams that there is no god, we know his intimacy. We hold out our hands each day in innocence and knowledge to go on this walk, to receive this life, to taste this daily bread.

"And forgive us our debts, as we also have forgiven our debtors" (Mt. 6:12). One does not go forward in the spiritual life without forgiveness. The way is strewn with the wreckage of wounded and wounding relationships. If we are still caught in emotional immaturity, we go careening off the royal way of fidelity to God by lavishing our love on the next attractive person, whatever the content of that attraction may be. In that wreckless ride, we give and receive hurts which cloud the soul in violence, self-pity, and revenge. If we are caught in the pharisaic love of the first place, that is, in ambition and the competition that accompanies it, we also wound and get wounded in our false ascent. The memory of the soul gets filled with images it cannot forget. Friends in the way of our climb become enemies. We become estranged from our brothers and sisters, because we are too busy supporting our own claims when we could be supporting theirs. The whole world becomes twisted when we cannot forgive our neighbors for getting in our way.

Our unforgiving ambition comes, however, from deeper wounds received in childhood. Even the most well-meaning parents pass on to their children unwillingly the learned ways of a world which, at best, must grow out of love for itself and into the love of God and, at worst, knows only survival from brutality. God has so ordained it that we begin in the womb of nature, helpless and totally dependent on our surroundings, so as to learn step by step to accept the gift of self, and in the storms of life, to give that life back to God who gave it.

In learning to take responsibility for our own life, we frequently find ourselves at a crossroad of forgiveness. As we unravel our past even back to childhood, we rediscover those wreckages along the road that need to be investigated. Who did this to us? How raw still is the wound? What was our part in the accident? The ancients have taught that in the time of prayer, the unsolved mysteries of our past come to haunt us. They will not let us go on the road of our spiritual lives because they keep us at the crossroads of forgiveness and block our way forward. If we read in our hearts the Scriptures which say: "The parents have eaten sour grapes, and the children's teeth are set on edge" (Jer. 31:29), and we believe that our misfortunes are someone else's fault, then we get sent back the way we came with vengeance in our hearts, or we veer off the road concocting philosophies about the sad nature of things. But if we read, "But all shall die for their own sins; the teeth of everyone who eats sour grapes shall be set on edge" (Jer. 31:30), then we sweep our hearts clean and are left pondering the mystery of evil that still may lurk there. The way forward is not to assign blame to others for our condition, but to acknowledge the sin and guilt that is our own, and to leave off the shame and fear that we have come falsely to accept and believe in. The way of forgiveness is the way beyond the crossroads. It begins with the forgiveness of others, parents, their parents, etc., but it extends to those who, caught in their own circumstances of unlove, did us harm. It stretches out to those who accept the lies of the evil one who has ruined our world. But in all of this extension, the way of forgiveness leads right back to ourselves. We have sinned deeply by refusing God, by stopping our ears to his voice, by wallowing in our own independence from God, all to our great calamitous diminishment. Can we forgive ourselves?

The monastic contemplatives know that only in a deep gift of prayer can we hold ourselves in forgiveness, and we can do this only in the womb of God's mercy. From here all forgiveness emanates. The urge to self-pity, clothed in a deep-seated self-righteousness, is for many at this stage of growth the last stumbling block on the royal way to God. Mirages of the old way of looking at things continually emerge. The clear way of faith often seems clouded. The voices that urge us to fall back onto secure ways of old thinking, especially in the close counsel of well-meaning friends, blunt the edge of our self-knowledge and forgiveness. So Job was constantly coaxed to reinterpret his situation to assign blame and curse God or, at least, find a way to let God off the hook of responsibility. But after we have forgiven ourselves, and after we have accepted completely the situation we are in, as Job did, we are still left to ponder the mystery of God and the mystery of why things are the way they are. Once we learn to forgive ourselves, the conundrum that bad things happen to good people melts away. None of us is good. We have all sinned and fallen short of the glory of God (Rom. 3:23). But once we accept the forgiveness of God, all of the bad things that happen to us, and to those we love, become blessings. These are difficult, no doubt, but they call us to seek greater understanding of God's will for us in Christ, his power, and his call through this passing world, and to trust him even through death to life beyond the grave.

If we cannot forgive ourselves, then we remain in our own false righteousness. We forget the weakness of our brothers and sisters. We forget the love of God who also accepted completely this situation of human ruin and came among us to bind our wounds by the oil of his own blood. Forgiveness stands and accepts the love of a forgiving God. God brings his mystery down from the clouds of the whirlwind of Job and into the human heart, which he took to himself in Jesus. Jesus preached the kingdom of God, which always has as its premise the forgiveness of God. Those who bring the kingdom into their hearts see that the leaders of this world are doomed to perish, that the faithful ones will eat and drink at Christ's table, and will sit on thrones judging the twelve tribes of Israel (see Lk. 22:30). They know how to interpret the signs of the times and will be the first to hear the trumpets announcing Christ's coming on the clouds. All of this is made possible by the knowledge and acceptance of God's forgiveness. Prayer that keeps open the door to God's forgiveness channels the kingdom of God into this world. Monastic contemplatives keep open this door for all of God's holy church.

"And do not bring us to the time of trial, but rescue us from the evil one" (Mt. 6:13). The desire for God now stands at the door of mystery. It has come to the edge of what it can know from experience. Desire can know no more. It must leave off and be carried unknowingly into communion with Jesus, the Son of God, and his mysterious self-offering to the Father. We fail to understand the situation of Jesus if we do not realize that it was the Spirit who carried him through the unwanted, unmerited and sacrificial death on the cross. Only in the Spirit can we interpret Jesus' cry in prayer that the chalice of suffering be taken away from him. Only in the Spirit can we understand the depths of Jesus' identification with us when he invoked the psalm which begins, "My God, my God, why have you forsaken me?" (Ps. 21[22]:2). The mystery of Christ finds its most precise definition in the agonized passage between death and life. In the womb of the Holy Spirit, where Christ tastes death and is raised in glory, the new creation is born in his risen body, beyond pain, tears, and tœ146he death which finite life must undergo. Everything in this new creation rejoices in the freedom of the Spirit, which now begins his ecstatic movement of return to the Father.

We can approach this final stage of the Mystery of Christ only in the power of the Holy Spirit. In the Spirit, our baptismal grace comes to full flower. We are joined to Christ in his passage between death and life. Our own passage becomes his passage. His passage encompasses our own.

The final struggle against the lies and snares of the evil one who fights furiously at the end is no longer our struggle. Our ship lies safe in the port of the Holy Spirit. The battle is joined by powers greater than we. It rages bitterly while we are only barely conscious of it. In each individual who stands in faith at the passage between death and life, the mystery of Christ is applied by the grace of Baptism. We become passive to the work of the Spirit who inserts us into Christ's own passage from death to life, the last cataclysmic contest between Christ and sin and death.

The Spirit prepares us for this mystery by long periods of grace and preparation. The journey of the spiritual life winds inevitably through straighter paths until we are able to pray in the Spirit the last petition of the Lord's Prayer. It is no longer we who pray it but we learn to pray it in Christ who invites us to shelter ourselves under his wings, the arms of the cross. At the end, we do nothing but rest in Christ. We know the weakness of our own efforts. We have learned to reach out to the Spirit who takes us through this last, most frightening journey. We would never take this journey on our own. The boldness and even reck-lessness of our faith empowers us to be in the Spirit and with Christ. The final journey is the fulfillment of our desire for God. It is our passage from partial knowing, as if seeing in a mirror dimly, to communion in the Spirit through Christ to the Father (see 1 Cor. 13:12).

Monastic contemplatives pray the Lord's Prayer in its fullest meaning. They fill up the content of its power by their desire for God. The pure utterance of the Lord's Prayer brings our desire into the desire of God himself, in the unknowable movement of the relations between the Father, the Son, and the Holy Spirit. In few words, with no empty phrases, and in full confidence that the Father is drawing us back to himself in the Spirit of Christ, we pray the words Our Savior gave us.

New York City
Feast of St. Agnes, January 21, 2006

ESSAY IV

Unity Viewed as Holiness

"That they may all be one. . . ." (Jn. 17:21a)

Introduction. Philosophers declare it. Religion proclaims it. The tendency we have to see the unifying principle wherever we look is brought to life by a liberal or theological education. Despite all the fragmentations in a wildly pluralistic society, the yearning for unity perdures among the thoughtful. Yet, for those engrossed in human affairs and beset as they are with the needs and unruliness of individuals, the idea of unity remains just that, an idea and the dream of those who muse. Yet ideas have a way of insinuating themselves in concrete reality even in triumphant fashion.

In this essay I shall discuss not the idea of the One explored by philosophers, nor the unity of all things by inclusivistic mystics, but the Christian prayer for unity voiced by Christ, ". . . so that they may be one, as we are one, I in them and you in me, that they may become completely one. . . ." (Jn. 17:22-23). The roots of the Christian liturgy support the notion of a converging oneness, while the behavior of the churches, which celebrate the liturgy, universal and local, often deny it. Investigation into these notions will raise questions whose answers will focus more and more on Christ, the One Son of the Father, sent to save humankind through the Spirit and in the Spirit. The goals of the philosophers and the mystics may seem similar to the contemplation of God the One and the Three. But where so many desires for unity remain unfulfilled yearnings or predictions, the journey narrated here will be one of the Christian experiences of God drawing individuals to himself in the mystery of his Oneness.

Jesus' prayer for unity begins to be realized in the individual when, through the operative grace of baptism, a person works to build an openness of spirit in whatever sphere he or she works. Instead of building barriers of selfishness, ambition, fear, or party spirit, the graced person coaxes others out from behind their barriers and refuses to participate in the erection of new ones. Charity is the virtue we use to name this positive activity, but unity is its effect and becomes an agent for higher integration, both personal and ecclesial. In this sense, it is a holiness. Remembering the Second Vatican Council's "universal call to holiness," we acknowledge that unity is the birthright of all the baptized. As they claim it, they move forward closer and closer to God and discern new insights into his mystery.

What is said here about the mystery of God is not a scrutiny of God's majesty, as if we could crudely penetrate that mystery in itself. Rather, it is a growing and gifting love and knowledge of God in his purpose for us. It is an experience and a transformation. As we come to love and know God in his saving will, we begin to participate in that saving will for others because we are mysteriously becoming divine ourselves in Christ and, finally, carried toward the Father in his Spirit. Therefore, union with God is the ultimate holiness in the Christian journey.

Unity remains an idea, not fulfilled in the concrete, until God gives the gift of it through his Spirit. We try to come to it through our own wisdom and we get rebuffed. The only way forward is to penetrate the Scriptures to discover God's wisdom. Often hidden behind difficult passages, hard to accept, wisdom reveals, by living it, glimpses of the salvific purpose of God. We are confronted with more questions and greater mysteries until we can go no further. We discover to our dismay, but are also aware of a distant recognition (that of the tree of life [see Gen. 2:9]), that the journey comes to a halt at the cross.

Christ, as he dies on the cross, stands revealed as the final judgment/mercy of God. All come to him, and those who wish to live go forward with him into new life, a life of manifold wisdom and diversity, but always verging toward greater unity, with Christ as the unifying factor.

I will ask why, with such a glorious and attractive holiness, the church fails so often to point to it, to preach it, and to find it.

Where can we locate this holiness in the church, since it must carry the promise of Christ that it be one? The church always knows itself to be one, holy, catholic and apostolic according to the creed it professes. Where in the church can we affirm this truth to be not just a kerygma, but an experience that can be narrated, so that others may find it?

As the faithful move forward in their parish life, they know how by their preaching and example they are apostolic. Ecclesial communities know, when they celebrate the Eucharist without respect of persons, that they are catholic. Indeed, all over the world, the apostolic activity of the church becomes its catholicity when people of "every tribe and language" celebrate the one and the same Eucharist. The church, as the very Body of Christ, is holy. Yet Christ's gift of his Spirit means that we, too, the individuals in that Body, are offered his holiness. But it is only received by living his Gospel. Yet where is the unity of the People of God? Is it to be found merely in an organizational unity stemming from the Vatican? Then what about the Christian East? What about other ecclesial communities? And how do we understand ourselves to be one with the non-Christian religions? And what about those who profess no faith, for whatever reason? They are all God's children and we pray for them as such: "In mercy and love unite all your children wherever they may be" (Roman Liturgy: Eucharistic Prayer III). The answer must lie in finding Christ, the source of all unity, at a deeper level than our ecclesial complacency allows.

Many of the faithful find the way forward into the life of the Gospel to be obscure, too difficult, with no one to lead them or to show them the way. Indeed, there are a few strong and graced individuals who break through the impasse of the cross by their own suffering and kenosis. These we call saints. But for most of us, the wisdom of God is an invisible mystery. All we see are the nonsense and foolishness of letting others win, while we ourselves continually lose.

In order to help break through the stumbling block of our wisdom, Christ's Spirit has gifted the church with the monastic tradition, so that the full heritage of Christ can be claimed by as many as choose to embrace it. For in monasteries faithful to the ascetic tradition, the full way of Christ is illumined so that all may see it. Monastic communities stand at the juncture where the wide net of the church's apostolic activity closes in on Christ, the narrow way, at once the judgment and mercy of God. The growing narrowness is what people fear. To the extent that they have been reduced to Christ in his suffering and death, and clothed with his teaching, the monks and nuns stand quietly, lovingly, at this crossroads of hope and frustration. By the witness of their lives, they move the faithful along the way. By their discourse and availability, they make palatable and sensible the strong words of the Gospel. By their withdrawal and separation from parish life, they are able to warn others of the real meaning of things ecclesial, for they stand as a prophetic witness against all that is unworthy of the church. They offer a gentle but urgent invitation to the faithful to avoid delay and to make haste toward Christ, who waits for us at the end of our lives and at the end of time, to bring us to the Father. He alone holds the mystery of the One (". . . no one knows the Father except the Son and anyone to whom the Son chooses to reveal him . . ." [Mt. 11:27]). Only through, with, and in him can we pray to the Father that all of us, in the same union which enfolds Father, Son and Holy Spirit, may be one.

The Unity of the Liturgy. "How wonderful are the works of the Spirit, revealed in so many gifts! Yet how marvelous is the unity the Spirit creates from their diversity . . ." (Roman Liturgy: Preface for Christian Unity). The liturgical year presents the church with a plethora of theological themes. It elaborates the mystery of Christ according to his historical coming—the Immaculate Conception of his Mother, the announcement of his birth, baptism, passion, death, resurrection, and ascension, and the sending of his Spirit. It divides these historical happenings into two great cycles, the Advent-Christmas-Epiphany cycle and the Lent-Easter-Pentecost cycle. The liturgy then goes on to reflect on the dogmatic consequences of these cycles. It celebrates the mystery of the Trinity, the beginning and the end of the Christ event. It dwells on the tender love and compassion of Christ in the feast of the Sacred Heart. It glorifies the Real Presence in the Feast of Corpus Christi. When not in the midst of these two great cycles, the church "orders" the Christian life of waiting for Christ to come in glory. By the Liturgy of the Word during this Ordinary Time, the church teaches the Gospel. It structures this in-between time around the teaching, signs and miracles of the Savior and fills the People of God with hope while it never ceases to participate in the heavenly Liturgy of Christ's Glory. His blessed Mother, so directly involved in the Christ event so as to be part of that mystery, with all her privileges and virtues, is taken up by the liturgy. Next comes the cycle of apostles to whom the full Revelation of Christ was given. In them "the message goes forth to all the earth" (Ps. 18[19]:4). Those most closely adhering to Christ down the centuries, so that they offer their lives to him in martyrdom, follow. The pilgrims of the narrow way, who left everything as they heard the call of Christ in the church to come follow him according to a monastic/religious rule are close behind. Finally, all the saints, whom the church calls holy in the grace of Christ, round out the liturgical year.

The diversity of the liturgy emanates from the manifold wisdom of Christ in the elaboration of his mystery. In past centuries, the Roman, Milanese, Mozrarabique (in Spain), Frankish liturgies, and others, contributed their cultural tendencies and insights to the prayers and styles of the sacraments, especially the Eucharist. The declines, the reforms, the Reformation and the Counter-Reformation have left their decisive features on the liturgy. Through the centuries, the liturgy has become like a rare prism, refracting so many rays of insight on Christ which shine on the faithful for their conversion and edification. But in the inevitable sclerosis of human time, the styles from all these modifications and emphases, and their paraphernalia, have obscured the mystery of Christ. The Scriptures become dark and unlovely since they are no longer taught, and the palpable trappings of triumph and pomp, beauty and ritual, come to substitute for the message of conversion to Christ in the Scriptures, and his beckon to greater participation in his offering to the Father. In many places and in many hearts, the reception of Holy Communion is not prepared for and focused by the liturgy but becomes an end in itself, since its obvious power and meaning seem to be able to stand alone. The consolation and the challenge of the entire eucharistic celebration, that is, to go and be Christ in ourselves and our world until he comes, goes unheeded in the noise of our own needs and desire for concrete feelings of love and approbation as we receive Holy Communion. We take to the tabernacle, unable to believe that, as we leave the church building, he is in us for the salvation of the world. We become like the Israelites who, when they returned to their homes from the temple, fell into worship of household gods because their religious faith in the Lord, who always seemed absent, was too weak. We indulge in misunderstandings of the Eucharist as only the presentation of the Real Presence, instead of the dynamic, grace-filled sacrament that constitutes the People of God. When we tire of the tabernacle, we go to the saints and multiply their novenas. We rely on our natural feelings of motherhood and all its complex psychological ties in our devotion to the Blessed Mother, as we wrench it from the Mystery of Christ. In all this, we fail to hear the warnings of the Scriptures to pray always so that religious faith in God may remain strong and that the spirit, which is willing, may bolster the flesh which is weak. In the marvelous elaboration of the mystery of Christ and his Body, the church, God has used every means to call us to conversion. He has turned everything into a means of salvation and has invited us to bring it to the Eucharist to be offered through, with, and in his Christ, so that everything may be redeemed. But, because of our psychological and bodily weakness, the sense of the spiritual call to be the noble People of God in the Eucharist becomes obscured and debilitated. Even in so-called sacred things, the mystery of Christ can remain hidden and, therefore, the unity of the liturgy is lost.

The church has tried to restore this sense of the mystery of Christ in the celebration of the liturgy by highlighting the four liturgical presences of Christ: in the presider, in the assembled People of God, in the Scriptures, because they are the very Word of God, and in his Real Presence in the sacred species of the bread and wine become his body and blood. None of the first three can be neglected if the full and correct meaning and effectiveness of the Real Presence is to be realized. Immediately, one sees that a dynamic religious faith must be brought to bear on these presences. The presider may or may not be inspiring. The Scriptures must be studied and prepared outside of the liturgy, and this is perhaps the most important ministry beyond presiding for the ordained minister: to prepare the people to celebrate the Eucharist by opening the Scriptures to their minds and hearts. And their second most important task must be the faith formation of the People of God, so that they know who they are and what they are celebrating when they approach the Eucharist. The Holy See and the bishops' conferences have spent much time and labor on these issues since the Second Vatican Council. We examine and seek to improve our seminaries to educate the presiders. We do not hesitate to employ the admirable scriptural exegesis at our disposal. We initiate adult catechetical classes and programs. We teach and teach again the church's understanding of the Real Presence and its proper devotions. What can bring these presences together so that the church may be vivified? What can unite and inspire the People of God so that the re-evangelization of the world can proceed? What can turn Catholic religious observance and legislation from a preoccupation with itself? Who can restore to the church the conviction that the time is short before Christ will come again to claim his own, those who have heard his word, lived by it and preached it to the four corners of the world?

The answer to these questions must lie in a return to fundamentals or, to the one fundamental, the Christ. He is first and preeminently with us in his church, his Body. There his Spirit gathers us in the Eucharist, and we have memory of him by the Scriptures, especially the Gospels. There, he teaches us how he lives among us through his Spirit, and how we, too, must live like him. But, in order to understand the Gospel teaching, the church provides us with an interpretative tool in the First Reading, usually from the Old Testament. The First Reading puts the Gospel teaching in the full light of God's overall salvific plan. We can be sure that when the faithful listen to the Scriptures with love, Christ's Spirit is there to teach them how all the Scriptures speak of him (see Lk. 24:25-27; 44). In our assemblies, therefore, the Scriptures pour out upon us the memory of Christ so that we may celebrate the sacraments, especially the Eucharist. But we must hear the Word before we can believe in the privileges of the sacraments. St. Paul provides the formula:

And how are they to believe in one of whom they have never heard? And how are they to hear without someone to proclaim him? And how are they to proclaim him unless they are sent? As it is written, "How beautiful are the feet of those who bring good news!" (Rom. 10:14-15).

The secret of the full participation in the Eucharist, the Body and Blood of Christ, lies in the preaching of the Word. The challenge, therefore, is to return to the Scriptures so that their full content of the living memory of Christ can be proclaimed. So much of preaching falls short of the prophetic Word. Sometimes it represents merely the preoccupation of the preacher, how he feels, what his opinions are, what he thinks other people should do, or how they should think or act. Apparently, his preaching comes from a vacuum where the Scriptures simply are not. If he neither reads the Scriptures, nor prays with them, nor sees himself as a humble spokesperson of their voice, then, in the eucharistic assembly, all that is left is himself. The sadness of this vacuum is unspeakable.

Sometimes the preacher feels the necessity of a constant, positive response to his homily. Afraid of the people, he prefers to please them, to lower the Word to their behavior and to their sense of justice, and, finally, to accept the notions of the prevailing culture. In this, at best, he feeds the people milk instead of solid food, pablum instead of steak. In a sense, he tacitly supports the status quo, the veneer of civility that covers unredeemed thoughts and actions, the tendency to quarrel and to seek for retribution. These, according to St. Paul, are human inclinations, not worthy of the more spiritual food that is the preaching of Christ (see 1 Cor. 3:1-4).

Sometimes a talented preacher may deliver a good sermon, well thought out, cohesive, compelling and memorable. Yet, if the words of his sermon are not a homily, that is, are not subservient to the Readings for the celebration, the wisdom of the preacher goes afloat, untethered to the Christian mystery and calling the people's attention to itself. This constitutes a direct attack on what the Spirit is trying to do in the liturgy. But a preacher who stands humbly as a mouthpiece of the Spirit fulfills his duty to break the bread of the Word of God for the feeding of the People of God.

How does the preaching of the Word support the unity of the liturgy? The answer lies in the desire for the mystery of Christ. From the very beginning of the celebration, we are about one thing, the memory of Jesus. The Holy Spirit, Christ's Spirit, brings about this memory, since the Spirit is about one thing, the declaration, in presence and action, of all that is of Jesus (Jn. 16:12-15). Since we are taught that Christ is present in so many ways in the liturgical celebration, we must listen to what he says in the Scriptures. The Spirit sharpens our listening when we are gathered together, so that everything in the Scriptures may speak of the Christ. No matter how obscure or tangential the feast of the day may seem to us, it is up to the presider to draw together the various strands of devotional meaning into a cohesive presentation of the Christ event. The presider may not shrink from this task, no matter how difficult. The admirable exegesis available to him and the multiple aids to preaching at his fingertips can help him in what must be his personal encounter with Christ in the Scriptures. In this, he becomes an instrument of the Holy Spirit. He must share with the People of God that which the Spirit puts in his mind and heart, so as to offer to the faithful the full fruit of the sacrament, and to exercise to the utmost his ordination to the ministerial priesthood. His work will be made so much easier if he has prepared or seen to the preparation of the People of God. Obviously, we are speaking here of a ministry that is comprehensive and demanding.

At a time when more and more parish administration and sacramental ministry fall on fewer priests, the proper preparation of the People of God to celebrate the Eucharist fittingly seems to take a back seat. The answer to this perennial problem may be a reordering of priorities in the lives of the ordained. By arrangements of parish staff, delegations to those qualified, by conferences, parish meetings, spiritual direction, proper parish rules, etc., the pastor/presider may adopt a keen spiritual insight into the spiritual needs of the parish. By his overseeing ministry, he may open the ears of the faithful so that they can hear what the Spirit is saying to the churches. Undoubtedly, it is a word of correction, of conversion, of compunction of heart, of soul-searching and lament, of celebration and discovery of the Christ. All of this spadework on the heart makes the self-offering of the faithful more and more effective as the liturgy of the Eucharist begins. The People of God have been gathered in the power of the Spirit. They have been prepared to worship God in spirit and in truth by that same Spirit. And now, still in the Spirit, they are joined to Christ, with the grace of their Baptism shining brightly, so that their own self-offering may proceed together with Christ's own sacrifice to the Father. And in this is God glorified. And we are fulfilled in our deepest thirsting for being beyond even what we taste of our own personhood. As we participate in the Body and Blood of Christ, we partake of the heavenly banquet, a banquet at one and the same time, a summit of the Christian life and a source for further growth in the Spirit. The presider, the faithful, the Scriptures, and the participation in the Body and Blood of Christ all conspire by the power of the Spirit to change our lives again and again so as to put on Christ, not just while in church, but much more importantly, in the living of our lives.

The celebration of Easter, source and summit of the liturgical year. "Father, accept this offering from your whole family and from those born into the new life of water and the Holy Spirit, with all their sins forgiven" (Roman Liturgy: 'Hanc Igitur' for Easter, from Eucharistic Prayer I). The unity of the liturgy can only be understood by its roots in the Easter event. For every celebration of the sacraments, and, especially the Eucharist, harkens back to the passion, death and resurrection of the Christ. We have filled the world with eucharistic celebrations. Yet they are all one. The Easter celebration, at the end of the Paschal Triduum, is present in every eucharistic celebration. Every Sunday celebration is another Easter, for there the faithful gather to remember the Lord's resurrection, and to break the bread and drink the cup in his memory. Each great liturgical cycle derives its meaning from the Easter celebration. Even the Incarnation looks forward to its fulfillment in the Paschal Triduum. Daily celebrations, in their turn, come from and look forward to the Sunday celebration. The preaching of the Word in the eucharistic celebration must point to the mystery of Christ in order to hold together in unity the manifold liturgical development inspired by the People of God in their love of and their devotion to Christ.

Yet there is a deeper, underlying purpose to the unity of the liturgy. The illumination that all things in the liturgy point to Christ and have him as their end extends to the whole world, its creation, and our place in it. If the Holy Spirit makes present and acting the memory of Christ in the sacramental celebrations of the church, it is only because the same Spirit has rolled out the whole of the economy of salvation for the Christ event. As God creates the world, it is a wind from God or, as the church has constantly interpreted it, the Spirit of God, which sweeps over the waters of chaos, bringing to being the things that are. Yet, right at the beginning, all the things of creation came to be through God's Word, the Christ, and "without him, not one thing came into being" (Jn. 1:3). We can take this to mean that God's purpose in creation is to celebrate his Word, eventually to be revealed as his Christ.

God's Spirit, beginning with creation but continuing on with every appearance God makes to Abraham, Isaac, Jacob, and the formation of his people, Israel, constantly looks forward to the mission of making Christ present for the salvation of the world. Every angelic manifestation, every inspiration of the prophets, every jot and tittle of the Law declares the glory of God in his Christ. He is the entire purpose and meaning of God's sending of the Spirit. The Spirit overshadows Mary and she conceives the Christ. The Spirit descends upon Christ at his Baptism, drawing down the blessing and affirmation of the Father. The Spirit drives Christ into the wilderness and prepares him for his ministry of calling out and defeating the evil of the world, and forming his Body, the church, around the apostolic community. The Spirit inspires Christ to set his face to go to Jerusalem, there to be taken up through suffering and death into his glory (see Lk. 9:51). Christ breathes forth his Spirit upon his gathered apostles on the evening of his resurrection (see Jn. 20:22-23). As he leaves the world in a physical way, he remains present and acting in it by his Spirit.

The Spirit gathers together the church and teaches its members all things and reminds them of all that Christ has said to them (Jn. 14:25-26). The Spirit continues his mission by making Christ present and acting, concrete and particular, in every gathering of the church. The world cannot receive him, because the Spirit is too subtle. "It neither sees him nor knows him" (Jn. 14:17). But the church knows him because he abides with us and will be with us. St. Paul puts it succinctly: ". . . no one can say 'Jesus is Lord' except in the Holy Spirit" (1 Cor. 12:3). The Spirit throughout the economy of salvation always identifies the Son, and his every action is to raise up Christ in the hearts of believers.

Yet his work is not complete until we participate in the glorification of the Christ. As we are transformed into Christ through his power, and become one with Christ, we find ourselves swept along in a new manifestation of the salvific economy. It is a revelation not deduced by the scientific scrutiny of the Scriptures, as we try to balance this text against that one, but an experience of truth, reserved to those in whom the Spirit is freely at work, and in whose hearts the Scriptures are opened. For now we are in the Spirit, completely at one with his mission of revealing Christ and uniting us to him. Having been baptized into Christ by the power of the Spirit, we begin our real return to the Father in the Spirit through Christ. It is through Christ, because he is our means of approach to God.

The Spirit remains a mystery. We are not united to him as we are to Christ. But we are totally his instruments as he continues his mission from the Father. The Spirit, having rolled out the economy of salvation in Christ, now folds it back, with all those for whom Christ died, into the Father. A more living, dynamic experience of the Three Persons could not be described. Yet, it is all in the Scriptures, as interpreted for us by the Spirit of God, so that we may properly understand the world in which we live by God's mercy. The Easter event, which announces and begins the joyful return to God of the People of God constitutes the unity of the liturgy. There the Spirit identifies the Christ, the object of the Father's love in the mystery of his coming among us. The Spirit identifies Christ as the risen Son of God in every act of the church and in all of creation which waits for redemption in the church. The Spirit holds the secret of the unity of all things in Christ.

"The waters saw you, O God, the waters saw you and trembled" (Ps. 76[77]:16a). The church, celebrating the Eucharist and the other sacraments, proclaims the unity Christ calls for. It effects that unity by the grace of the sacraments. It provides the guide to exercise that grace by the Scriptures, even the hard saying of the Gospels, which the Spirit interprets for the church. How do we become part of the river of unity that flows in the midst of the church on its way back to God? How do we discern the work of the Spirit who wills to submerge us in that river of unity so that we may rise out of it with new, spiritual senses? The answer must lie in the heart of the church, in the very middle of the sacramental stream of the mystic Jordan River in which all is made holy in the Baptism of Christ.

From his Baptism by John to his suffering and death in Jerusalem is one movement, affirmed by the Father when he said, "You are my Son, the Beloved; with you I am well pleased" (Mk. 1:11b). The Spirit, descending on him like a dove from the shattered heavens, continues to hover over him, giving purpose, meaning, and identification to this journey from the Baptism event until his death on the cross (see Mk. 1:10b). In this movement of the Spirit, the embrace of all things except sin is accomplished in him. As the Scriptures say: "For we do not have a high priest who is unable to sympathize with our weaknesses, but we have one who in every respect has been tested as we are, yet without sin" (Heb. 4:15). The Spirit plunges Jesus deep into the waters, there to affirm his human condition. But as Jesus rises from the waters, the theophany occurs from which he will begin his public ministry of teaching and signs so that all may believe in him. From this time on, the elements become pliant to his touch in miracles of healing and signification, so that at his glorification we, too, may know his healing through the sacraments which he has passed on to his church. From then on, the preaching of the Christ as the Word of God becomes infused with power. As St. Paul declares: "For we know, brothers and sisters beloved by God, that he (Christ) has chosen you, because our message of the gospel came to you not in word only, but also in power and in the Holy Spirit and with full conviction . . ." (1 Th. 1:5).

From one kind of lowliness and poverty of condition, that is, the full assumption of our human condition, Jesus passes to a kenosis of the Spirit's doing, that of obedience to the Father unto death. In this second phase of emptying, Christ is revealed as the Son of Man, making his way to Jerusalem, drawing all to himself, and speaking and acting for all creation. In his humanity/divinity, he subsumes everything to himself so that the death he embraces is the death of corruption, loss, pain, fear, guilt and shame. All that is not worthy of him dies with him. What remains is a clean and uncluttered way to God which only the Son of Man could effect in our own bodies as well as the whole creation. His church becomes the universal sign of the way to God and throws out both the wide net of preaching and the narrow way of the cross about which he taught us. Beginning with his Baptism, therefore, he summons the whole world and, by his voice, awakens it to its spiritual destiny. By his miracles of healing, he defies the powers of darkness, engages them, and calls them out to a final confrontation. By his suffering, death, and resurrection, in a second completely unexpected turn which surprises the evil one hungry to devour him, he brings down the devil with him to his own death and breaks forever his power. In him, our world is not only summoned but also called together from the ruins of its evil fragmentation into a unity that once again orders it as when God first created it, and one that offers it the possibility of transformation into the new and eternal creation willed for it by God from the beginning (see Eph. 1:3-10). In the two movements of the Christ event, the choice for God and his unity and transformation in Christ are offered to the world and to each of us, now and every day of our lives. As the Psalmist sings: "O that today you would listen to his voice! Harden not your hearts . . ." (Ps. 94[95]:7d-8a).

"Repair what is shattered for it sways" (Ps. 59[60]:4b). But we have hardened our hearts. The unity Christ willed for his church lies in ruins. The grand vocation of the church to be the sign of unity in a fragmented world has yet to be fulfilled. Our minds, conscious of how we have not lived the sacramental graces received, and chastened by the Scriptures, are directed to the debacle of Christian division. Not for this did Christ die, rise and enter the hearts of his faithful. Not for this did the Spirit extend the mercy of God in the Law, the Psalms and the Prophets. Not for this did God create the universe. The burden of chaos in the Christian world weighs heavy on every faithful heart. Yet, the solution to the problem probably does not lie so much in universal initiatives that might bring together the various Christian communities. These ecumenical endeavors are salutary and good, and we wait for them with patience and longing. But the church, gathered together by the Spirit, responds to God's initiatives in every local assembly. Even when the universal church seems preoccupied with disciplinary, doctrinal or organizational problems, or when, God forbid, it is taken up with things not of the

Gospel, the Holy Spirit raises up the memory of Christ in pockets here and there throughout the church. There, the beginnings of unity may be discovered. There, will the turn-around from chaos to order be discerned. Not so much by programs will this growing unity be achieved, but by the conviction of a shared grace on the part of each gathered assembly. For they are gathered by the same Spirit and, in truth, they begin to look across denominational lines to one another, not in suspicion or hate but in love and in mutual respect for the gifts poured out on each of them. The Second Vatican Council intuited this growing power of unity when it declared that the grace found in each ecclesial community is the same grace of the same Holy Spirit, given in various measures.[1] Our way is then clear to look across the aisles, the streets, the cultures and the ages to all our brothers and sisters who believe in and worship the Christ. In their eyes, we see him. For there we identify in the Spirit the one who loved us and died for us, so that we may be one with him in the Father. Even as we do so, we may discern remedies for our own ecclesial problems.

At a time when Roman Catholic preaching was probably never at a lower ebb, the way forward to a renewed church, if I have intuited the issue properly, is precisely through a restored tradition of preaching. Our brothers and sisters of the Reformed tradition have honored the Word before all else. Could we not imbibe something of their emphasis, without compromising the fullness of our belief in the sacraments? Do they not have exactly what we need to find the grace that has been liberally poured out upon us but which we have studied and locked up in libraries, that is, the very Word of God itself? At a time when the beauty and dignity of worship has been drained out of our Roman Catholic liturgy in the pursuit of full participation by the faithful, can we afford to continue the maintenance of divisive walls against the Christian East, where the poetry and style, born of a refined sensibility of things both theological and liturgical have never been forgotten? We are not Easterners, and we can never be. But rather than seeing ourselves as opposites, which is true

---

[1] Decree on Ecumenism, *Unitatis Redintegratio*, Vatican Council II, vol. 1, The Conciliar and Postconciliar Documents, ed. Austin Flannery, OP (Costello Publishing Company, Northport, NY, 1998), n.3, pp. 455–456.

enough, could we not begin to inculcate into our own experience the riches we find lining our borders? Is this not the way the Western tradition built itself up through the ages? Is not the Western Christian tradition a fecund marriage of things Roman with things Slovakian, Germanic, Frankish and Moorish?

In our democratization of the liturgy, highly laudable and never to be rejected, we have forgotten that the mysteries of our faith rely on the worthiness of the human means to convey them. Language, art, music, architecture, gesture, and attitude need to come from our best efforts as human beings or risk the banality of the lowest common cultural denominator. The easy solution to this in Roman Catholic circles is to backtrack in time and place to liturgical practices that carried the mysteries in the more recent past, to the time when we or our parents and grandparents were children. Those traditions basked in the warm light of the 19th-century European Roman Catholic revival as it made its way to foreign shores in the 20th century. There, strong, ethnic Catholicism protected and gave consolation to uprooted populations. Its traditions were fixed in time, place and political realities that in the present no longer obtain. Now they are broken by the power of the Spirit speaking through the Second Vatican Council as it urged the church to adapt itself to a new global situation. Former cultural, liturgical and even theological expressions of belief can no longer speak in a completely adequate way the mysteries which have been carried forward in time in the course of salvation history by the Holy Spirit. Past traditions, born of and for a particular time and place, cannot substitute for the slow and painful growth that new liturgical, cultural expressions require for maturity. This is not to say that the rich storehouse of Roman Catholic liturgical tradition is not to be opened. But it is to declare that a mere return to the past, in a way that denies what the Spirit is saying to the churches, is to block the progress of the church, not to enhance it. From our neighbors—the East, the Reformed, the Separatist and the Baptist/Evangelical— viewed with love, we will find the way forward with new ideas, fresh reflections and renewed cultural acuity. New wine must be stored in new wineskins, or else what is new, rising and fermenting will burst the skins which are old (see Mt. 9:17).

With full confidence in the love of God poured out for us in the blood of Christ, we also look around us to those who are not of our belief, or who have rejected the church because of hurtful experiences. Instead of seeing differences, rejection, animosity and derision in their faces, we are empowered to look rather for courtesy, kindness, mutual agreement and common cause. To be sure, in some there will be a spurning and a dismissal of all things Christian and of all things connected to religion. Yet, we have the teaching of our Christ to turn the other cheek, to go the extra mile, to refuse the power of evil and unbelief and to face the other with the conviction that here is one who is also called. The missionary activity of the church begins with this conviction, if there is to be any headway at all with those who do not believe or who have been scandalized.

The example supported by the Vatican in the approach to non-Christian religions is salutary. On the level of theology, philosophy and doctrine, we are far removed from Hinduism, Buddhism, Confucionism, etc., in their various forms. Yet, in the realm of experience, the monastic orders of all religions come very close to one another, and on that level we can dialogue, grow in mutual respect, and come close to one another in support, understanding and mutual upbuilding. Religious peoples at war with others over their truth claims exhibit an arrogance and immaturity that does not fit with our Savior's teaching. We remember the apostles' question to Jesus, when the Samaritans would not receive Jesus on his way to Jerusalem: "Lord, do you want us to command fire to come down from heaven and consume them?" But the Lord turned and rebuked them (Lk. 9:54-55b). Not only should we not rebuke others who do not believe along with us, but also we should recognize that no good or wholesome deed is outside of God. No behavior in harmony with the Gospel is condemned. No upright act goes unrewarded. Can we not extend to other religions the attitude of Christ when he said: "Whoever is not against us is for us?" (Mk. 9:40). Christ urges us on to recognize and affirm that which is good and true wherever we see it, especially in the religions of the world according to which billions of God's children live and die. Our belief in Christ, and in all the Father's revelation about him, will only grow stronger in the Spirit. We must respond to what has been revealed to us, and we must carry that response to the very depth of our being. It is from this depth that we can afford to come out of our parochialism and continue the mission of the Spirit to gather all into Christ. The mystery of how this unity is to be accomplished remains. But the call to act in the unity of the Spirit spurs us on to action.

The church also faces the enmity of the world culture and despite the great number of Christians, feels itself hemmed in and trapped by the all-pervasive attitudes of a foreign power. Here, again, the call to see and act on the unity of all things in Christ can overpower the roars and threats of our culture's animosity. It is all too easy for the church to condemn outright the actions of the secular world. It is a much more difficult thing to look with love into the red mouth of the monster and see in there the fear and entrapped anger of a diminished person. The triumph of convenience, selfishness and greed, so rampant in our culture, is only the opposite of the longing for fulfillment, the fear of pain and the dread of poverty. Despite the great lengths to which our culture has gone to articulate a godless society, despite short-sightedness and blindness of our leaders and influential people, despite the selfishness of those who are opportunistic and possessive or the hubris of those whose prominent position has led them to influence and sway positions in realms where they have no competence, and despite the folly and misery experienced by so many individuals who buy into this false way of life, there remains the image of Christ on everyone and on every work. "All things came into being through him, and without him not one thing came into being. What has come into being through him was life, and the life was the light of all people" (Jn. 1:3-4). Even from the actions of folly, God can and does draw good. We who believe in this must call out the goodness of life in every circumstance, even if it is a goodness gone bad. Somewhere in it God's redeeming work waits to be revealed. For there lies hidden behind every selfish act some longing for the freedom of self-sacrifice and the bright light of God in, through, and beyond this physical reality. As the Second Vatican Council reminded us in its decree *Gaudium et Spes*,

> . . . *the world which the Council has in mind is the whole human family seen in the context of everything which envelopes it: it is the world as the theatre of human history bearing the marks of its travail, its triumphs and failures, the world, which in the Christian*

vision has been created and is sustained by the love of its maker,
which has been freed from the slavery of sin by Christ who was
crucified and rose again in order to break the stranglehold of the
evil one, so that it might be fashioned anew according to God's
design and brought to its fulfillment.[2]

It is up to us to reveal and to manifest this design. The
so-called works of darkness lie open to the corruption of all
things temporal. Their power and their fury are here today and
gone tomorrow. But the actions of the Spirit, even in this passing
world, because they are all about Christ who has won the victory
over sin and death, are eternal.

The question remains: How do we set about restoring the
unity of the church? How do we join the graces received in the
sacraments to the ability to live the teaching of the Gospel? How
do we live in Christ so that we become like him and become
instruments of unity wherever we find ourselves in the church?

To descend with Christ into the waters of Baptism, that is,
into the depth of his own suffering, death and regeneration, is
to find in his eyes, his ears, indeed, all his senses the holiness of
all things, once they have been purified in his blood. Our purification occurs when we put on his Gospel teaching and go with
him into the Jordan of his Paschal Mystery. We are afraid to take
the plunge into deeper waters, into a deeper commitment of our
original baptismal grace, to be whirled about in seeming chaos
and mystery because such a dive renders us out of control and
foolish. The wisdom of the cross seems preposterous and dangerous. Our intellect can embrace the ideas from Jesus' teaching on
the Sermon on the Mount, as difficult as they are to live out. From
Levinas' proposals of hospitality in the 20th century,[3] all the way
back to Abel's murder by Cain, we recognize that the neighbor
is asked to cede pride of place to the other. Were there to be only
two persons on the entire earth, they would be in competition,

---

[2] Pastoral Constitution on the Church in the Modern World, *Gaudium et Spes,*
n. 1–3, pp. 903–905.

[3] Emanuel Levinas, *Entre-nous, On Thinking-of-the-Other,* trans. Michael B.
Smith, Barbara Harshav (Columbia University Press, New York, 1998), Author's
Preface, pp. XI–XIII.

one insisting on the dominance over the other. The Sermon on the Mount teaches us to cede to the neighbor this pride of place. To be a noble human being that can live in peace with his neighbor is, at least on the intellectual level, an attractive and desirable thing. But what we cannot accept so easily is what St. Paul will call the foolishness of the cross (see 1 Cor. 1:18ff). To be considered a fool for having thrown away one's own life for the sake of another is another question. That foolishness appears in Jesus' teaching where he enunciates the mystery of God's election. We turn to the hard sayings of the Gospels and inquire of them the way forward to the unity Christ prayed for.

". . . and sweeter are they than honey, than honey from the comb" (Ps. 18[19]:11bc). At the end of the public ministry of Jesus, and immediately before the passion narrative begins in the Gospel of Matthew, Jesus describes the last judgment:

> *When the Son of Man comes in his glory, and all the angels with him, then he will sit on the throne of his glory. All the nations will be gathered before him, and he will separate people one from another as a shepherd separates the sheep from the goats, and he will put the sheep at his right hand and the goats at the left. Then the king will say to those at his right hand, "Come, you that are blessed by my Father, inherit the kingdom prepared for you from the foundation of the world; for I was hungry and you gave me food, I was thirsty and you gave me something to drink, I was a stranger and you welcomed me, I was naked and you gave me clothing. I was sick and you took care of me, I was in prison and you visited me"* (Mt. 25:31-36).

When the righteous protest that they cannot remember doing any of these things directly to the Lord, he answers them, "Truly I tell you, just as you did it to one of the least of these who are members of my family, you did it to me" (Mt. 25:40). The lessons here are manifold. Jesus makes the absolute connection between people who profess him and himself. They are all one, and there is no division among them. What is done to any of them is done to Christ, and done to all. St. Paul poignantly experienced this identification between Christ and the church on his way to Damascus with threats and murder against the disciples there:

Now as he (Paul=Saul) was going along and approaching Damascus, suddenly a light from heaven flashed around him. He fell to the ground and heard a voice saying to him, "Saul, Saul, why do you persecute me?" He asked, "Who are you, Lord?" The reply came, "I am Jesus, whom you are persecuting" (Acts 9:3-5).

St. Paul will go on to include in his letters the doctrine of the Body of Christ, where the Spirit will unite the glorified Christ to all who are baptized in him in one indivisible entity which is called his very Body, so close is the relationship between Christ and his followers. The Spirit identifies this Body and continues as the principle of unity of the Body, so that there may be a variety of gifts all emanating from the same Spirit of Christ (see 1 Cor. 12:11-13; Eph. 1:23; Col. 1:18).

At the judgment, people will be looking for mercy if they are humble, or justice if they are proud. The goats find it hard to see the sheep invited into the kingdom prepared for them from the foundation of the world. They are incensed at the perceived injustice when they are told to depart from the king into the eternal fire prepared for the devil and his angels. They plead with the king for a hearing to state their case. "Lord, when was it that we saw you hungry or thirsty or a stranger or naked or sick or in prison, and did not take care of you?" (Mt. 25:44). But it is too late. They never made the connection between Christ and the lowly in the church. Even in their celebration of the Eucharist, they failed to take the Gospel teaching to heart. We can assume that the "eternal punishment" (Mt. 25:46) that awaits them is the constant gnawing thought that God's ways are not fair, not just, not clear. For if he had appeared to them in necessity as the great, sophisticated, beautiful and majestic God, surely they would have taken care of him.

The just, for their part, are surprised at the sweet taste in their mouths as they enter into the joy of the kingdom. For in their service of the poor and needy disciples, that is, the lowliest and the neediest in the church, whether theirs be a material poverty or a spiritual one, or, even by extension, the poor and needy of any of God's children, they carried the cross of Christ. They knew rejection and dissatisfaction, carping and the making of impossible demands, misunderstanding and ridicule, self-doubt and the agony of faith in what they were doing. Hearts get purified in this crucible. And the cross of Christ drips its sweet honey, the honey of eternal life, into their mouths and beings as they come to understand fully the service which they rendered. At the time, there was no reward, no honor, no affirmation, only the conviction of faith. The Father who saw all of this done in secret, will reward them with a taste of the cross of his Christ (see Mt. 6:2-4). For what was bitter is now sweet, and what was painful is now pleasure. This is the heritage of those who celebrate the Eucharist and find there the power to obey the Scriptures. They begin to taste the sweetness of the cross of Christ.

"Do all things without murmuring and arguing . . ." (Phil. 2:14). The lessons continue in the starkness of Jesus' teaching. In the Gospel of Matthew, in the parable of the laborers in the vineyard, our sense of God's apparent injustice grows to a loud crescendo. A landowner calls out workers to labor in his vineyard. The usual daily wage is agreed upon. But the landowner continues to hire workers throughout the day, for the same agreed-upon wage. At the end of the day, an equal amount gets paid out to the early risers as well as the latecomers. When those who had worked all day saw the inequality balanced against them,

> . . . *they grumbled against the landowner, saying, "These last worked only one hour, and you have made them equal to us who have borne the burden of the day and the scorching heat." But he replied to one of them, "Friend, I am doing you no wrong; did you not agree with me for the usual daily wage? Take what belongs to you and go; I choose to give to this last the same as I give to you. Am I not allowed to do what I choose with what belongs to me? Or are you envious because I am generous?" So the last will be first, and the first will be last* (Mt. 20:11-16).

Preaching on this Gospel passage is a chore since how do you explain the seeming arbitrary behavior of the owner of the vineyard? We cry, "Unfair." And we despise the good luck of the lazy ones who worked but one hour. We think of all those who get ahead by cunning rather than by hard work. We criticize immigrants for the opportunities they so quickly seize upon, while we and our parents and forebears labored to produce the bounty these newcomers are now enjoying. We are disdainful of those on welfare and the homeless, since we have all had the same opportunities, and they seem to choose not to utilize their gifts and talents. We are jealous of those in our own group whose luck, for we cannot see any other reason, has advanced them above us. We grumble against those in the workplace who cut corners and get away with it and even enjoy official favor, while we follow the straight and narrow path and, in our own hearts, maintain our superiority over them. We react to all of this supposed injustice by attitudes, subtle and overt, by prejudices that ooze out in unguarded moments, by our civil voting habits, and even by judgments on our children when they follow another path than the one we set for them. Why do we engage in these grumblings? Is it because we feel a diminishment of ourselves when others are chosen over us? Is it because we insist on our own justice based on this world's attitudes where we have placed our hope? Is it because when control of persons or situations is yanked out of our hands we feel that our sovereignty has been compromised and our power overthrown? For us who hold these attitudes, the election of the last over us, who see ourselves as the first and who have worked so hard to get there, is not only unacceptable but is a source of consternation and anger that may lead to the pride of revenge and retaliation.

The parable contains many levels. Certainly the most fundamental one has to do with the Gentiles as the latecomers, while the Israelites bore the day's heat of God's Word, the constant correction by the prophets, and the weight of the Law. For the Jews can say, "Who are these recently arrived who know nothing of the Hebraic tradition, who call themselves the People of God when that title is reserved for us, the Jews?" When it comes to Christians, we find the same kind of murmuring. We who know the traditions from childhood, despise those who revel in the Good News without knowing all the ancient practices and teachings that we know. Or, from our position on high in the church, we look down on the ignorant faithful who do not know their right hand from their left and cannot possibly be as close to God as we are who pray to him with the occult prayers and learned methods of our traditions. Yet the riches of the kingdom of heaven may just be poured out on those whom we despise rather than on ourselves who feel we deserve it. Perhaps, with the honor shown us and our position in the church, we have already received our reward. In all of this murmuring, we reveal ourselves as lacking in knowledge of the gifts God has given us. For we think that what we have accomplished is our own. We make ourselves into little gods, local and even universal potentates who have rights and privileges over against others and, therefore over against God himself. In so doing, we divide up the world by drawing boundaries, erecting walls and fortifications, and separating on our own authority the good from the bad into corrals of our own justice and righteousness. The fruit of complaining against the generosity of God when it is directed to others whom we do not approve is the fragmentation of the church, the international ecclesial community, and, of course, the human community itself.

God wills to topple every fortress that is not his own. His first commandment is: "I am the Lord your God, who brought you out of the land of Egypt, out of the house of slavery; you shall have no other gods before me" (Ex. 20:2-3). These other gods are often of our own making, and frequently they are we ourselves.

How shall we learn from this parable? How shall we rejoice with those who are placed ahead of us? The Spirit must show us the way, which is a way of reduction of our own possibilities, our own ambitions, our own desires, down to our essential being. At the bottom of ourselves, we find a featherless creature, crying, dependent, defenseless, and naked to the elements. God has had pity on us. In the wonderful, bold image of the Prophet Ezekiel (Ez. 16:1-34), God sees us in our nothingness, as he did the young girl, Jerusalem, in the lowliness of her origin and birth. As she was thrown out into the open field, an abandoned baby, so are we cast away from God's presence by our sins. The Lord passed by Jerusalem and saw her flailing about in her own blood. But the Lord said to her, "Live! And grow up like a plant of the field." The Lord says to each one of us, "Live! Be cleansed of your blood-sin by the clear waters of Baptism." Just as Jerusalem grew to be a great city, so we are endowed with all the gifts appropriate to our particular calling. Just as with Jerusalem, when the Lord waited patiently for her to grow up into full womanhood and the age for love, so it is with us. God waits for us to grow into the maturity of our calling, so that we can become generative in his church through our communion with him. All this is done by means of the gifts of his Spirit, who expands our horizons as the beauty of a girl blooms unexpectedly into the splendor of a handsome woman.

Yet, we neglect the constant thought of God in the business and importance of our lives. We fail to discern his presence, his Spirit, for he is subtle and avoids the crudities of our behavior. For his fruits are "joy, peace, patience, kindness, generosity, faithfulness, gentleness, and self control" (Gal. 5:22-23). We fall into a state of forgetfulness, and substitute for the gratitude we owe God the justice of a temporal world with no spiritual horizon. We become the laborers in the vineyard who complained to the Lord out of their own righteousness. And we hear the terrible rebuke, "Am I not allowed to do what I choose with what belongs to me? Or are you envious because I am generous?" (Mt. 20:15). We have become our own kings and queens, our own wayfarers and travelers consulting our own maps, and conclude in great forgetfulness that all our good things, and our desires and our ambitions come from our own power and need to be fulfilled on our own terms.

The reduction of our powers and the dismantlement of our fortifications is the work of the Spirit in our lives, all coming from the initial grace of Baptism. The Spirit grants us the humility to see anew our situation, to stop our grumbling, to let our hearts fill with the joy and love of the Lord, to taste the goodness that comes from a rededicated life. Yet, that is only the beginning. For the Spirit leads us deeper into the mysteries of God's election.

Not until we can rejoice at the gifts of another will we be justified in God's grace. We speak here of more than a tolerance of others, more than a comfortable, if half-hearted, accommodation. We should become like an older brother who actively worked to rehabilitate a ruined younger son. Just as the prodigal father took back his wayward child, so we, the older brother, can share in the father's joy and be the first to kill the fatted calf, the first at the father's right to receive the traveler and bask in the true light of the glory of forgiveness. How shall we welcome our brothers and sisters returning from their disastrous outward journey away from God? We shall climb to that place where God welcomes them, the cross of Christ. By our own imitation of Christ, by the immolation of all that we hold dear and sacred to our person, by the willing surrender of ideas, ambitions and birthrights will we climb the mount of the cross, join ourselves to him and die with him in order to become so united to him that we share in his glory, even as we still live on this earth. Then, and only then, will we gladly acknowledge the haggard penitents as well as the upcoming, fresh-faced newcomers to the vineyard. Only then will we notice the strangeness of the reply of the first laborer when he grumbled against the landowner. Secure in a confidence that sees beyond the world and its justice, we can afford to be generous, even foolishly so, with the abundance of this world, tethered as it is to eternal possessions. We can even afford to rejoice with those who rejoice in their newfound grace, though it be above anything we have received.

"And who is my neighbor?" (Lk. 10:29b). The Gospel teaching that best sums up the themes hard to bear that have been developed above occurs in the Gospel of Luke at the parable of the Good Samaritan (Lk. 10:25-37). The Samaritan exhibits an admirable array of qualities, all administered through his compassion for the man who had fallen in with robbers. He, a Samaritan, overcomes the obvious prejudice of his kind against the Jews, personified by the wounded man he encounters on the road to Jericho. What a priest would not do, nor a Levite, this Samaritan was willing to do, cost him what it may. He took charge of the situation, bandaged the man's wounds, loaded him onto his own animal and took him to an inn. One would think that appropriate charity would end there. Let others carry some of this burden. Instead, the Samaritan spent time overnight with the wounded man, gave the innkeeper more than sufficient funds to keep the unfortunate until his wounds should heal, and even offered to reimburse the innkeeper on his return should he spend more than the Samaritan left for his neighbor's care. What is appropriate here is defined not by what conventional charity would do, or what we would do and call generous, for, then, what the Samaritan did would be out of all bounds. The Samaritan did not consider himself, or what people would call fair and appropriate. He did what was entirely appropriate to the wounded man. It was exactly what he needed and more so. All of a sudden, the bright light of unity shines forth in the Samaritan's actions. He and the wounded man are made one. The innkeeper shares in this goodness. An event of brutality against the human person has been turned into a theophany illuminating the connections that unite all of us to God.

To an audience of Jews, this parable was aimed directly at their own ideas of holiness and religious duty. The parable raises the stakes to new heights which most of them, and also us, simply cannot accept. If this parable teaches me who is my neighbor, then clearly I must change the way I live. Everyone is my neighbor, everyone who puts a claim on my compassion. That means that I must live in a state of compassion all the time, even as the Scriptures exhort us to pray always and never lose heart (see Lk. 18:1). This compassion allows no room for comparisons, grumblings against what I don't agree with, complaints against those who are around me, the indulgence of party spirit when I am with my own kind, and the ultimate surrender, the control of my own environment where I protect myself against the gross intrusions of others. Compassion of the kind the Samaritan showed has one other impossible quality. He was overwhelmingly, inappropriately generous. There was simply no logic of duty or of calculation in his behavior. But he put himself in the shoes of the wounded man, and there he found what was appropriate to do. We have almost no human precedent of this that we can enshrine as our own. What the Samaritan did is too costly. We cannot embrace it. We cannot teach it or hand it on. But for an illumination of this generosity, we might look to parents who, out of love, give their lives in sacrifice so that their children might live. If only they would not exact a worthy payment for their early love in the later life of the child. The only other place to search is God's generosity when he offered his own Son for our redemption. The litany-like set of actions performed by the Samaritan, the first compassionate notice of the victim, the carrying of the wounded man on his beast, the agreement with the innkeeper, and the promise of more payment on his return, mounts up to an enormous height of ecstatic generosity. A similar kind of formula is to be found in the early christological hymn:

Let the same mind be in you that was in Christ Jesus,
Who, though he was in the form of God,
Did not count equality with God as something to be exploited,
But emptied himself, taking the form of a slave,
Being born in human likeness.

And being found in human form, he humbled himself

And became obedient to the point of death— Even death on a cross (Phil. 2:5-8).

But a Samaritan while traveling came near him. He went to him and bandaged his wounds, having poured oil and wine on them.

Then he put him on his own animal, brought him to an inn, and took care of him.

The next day he took out two denarii, gave them to the innkeeper, and said, "Take care of him; and when I come back I will repay whatever you spend" (Lk. 10:33-35).

In God's move toward us in his Son, there is no logic of superiority, no consideration of divinity, no preference for the kingdoms of this world, but, rather, a total and completely unexpected identification with the case of every human being without distinction, and a sacrifice of the worst and most brutal kind for the sake of all of us, the privileged as well as the trampled and suffering poor. This purpose of offering his Son for our redemption came from the depths of God's generous compassion for us, who were lost in our own mess. From deep within the Godhead, in a move of unspeakable love, the Father sent out the Spirit to prepare the way for the coming of his Son, to move him inexorably to Jerusalem and his crucifixion by the powers of this world, and to raise him up so that all of us may be offered newness of life in the same mode, all in the fullness of time.

Ecstatic generosity is the source of our existence and regeneration. This is God's way with us, from the mission of the Spirit to create the world according to the Word, the Son, to the mission of the Son, who comes to us in the flesh by the power of the same Spirit and sacrifices his life for us and brings down to death, death itself. The only way back to that source, and our own fulfillment, is to love God and our neighbor with the same kind of free abandon. The parable of the Good Samaritan teaches us that God is ready to infuse in us that same mind which was (is) in Christ Jesus, indeed, the same mind which is in his Spirit and in the Father himself. From the wide net of the church, we are invited to follow the narrow way, down and away from our pride and lies. There we encounter with compassion all the neighbors who claim our love and service. The narrow way continues on to that place of horror and suffering which is the Cross of Christ. Here is where all things stand united, caught in a demonstration of generous love that no one can gainsay. To this cross, all is reduced, for there is no boasting before God, no kingdom that can stand before the King on the cross. The Spirit of unity shepherds all of the elect to this place and empowers them out of love to join the Savior in the redemption his sacrifice effects. From this one place, all the rebirth of ourselves and our world begins. From this one place of unity emanates a plethora of good things, of gifts and possibilities, graces and strengths that people of the world would find dizzying, even in their worship of the seeming infinity of the splendor of the metropolis. The cross of Christ is indeed "foolishness to those who are perishing, but to us who are being saved it is the power of God" (1 Cor. 1:18).

"He will not cry or lift up his voice, or make it heard in the street; a bruised reed he will not break, and a dimly burning wick he will not quench . . ." (Is. 42:2-3ab). St. Paul goes on to say that God will destroy the wisdom of the wise and the discernment of the specialist. Where is the wisdom we seek? Where are the theologians who speak of this wisdom with their lives as well as in their writings? Where in the church can we find this narrow way that is more than words, teachings and occasional reflections? Where is the Spirit working in the church, the Spirit that flees from the proud and arrogant, the self-satisfied and those who are smug in their vapid traditions? How can we join ourselves to that stream of unity which the Spirit has caused to spring up in the church, that stream that since the glorification of Jesus begins to make its sure way back to the Father?

The answer is that the Spirit is causing this secret unity all over the church in the hearts of the simple and the pure who listen to the Word of God, celebrate the Eucharist with faith and hope, and give over their lives to listening and obeying the Scriptures. Yet so many of these individuals seek and need further guidance, for the way is narrow and steep. So many of them are shoulder to shoulder with others in the church who have no ears for the speech of eternal redemption. How can they find the encouragement to keep moving ahead with alacrity, to find eventually like-minded persons, to avoid counting the cost of their sacrifice, and, standing on the shoulders of others before them, to keep reaching to the "heavenly (upward) call of God in Christ Jesus?" (Phil. 3:14b).

A possible and concrete way of advance for those who are on their way to the heavenly kingdom is the ancient, but always new, monastic tradition. In its writings, its lives and its quiet witness in the church, it heralds the way of return for those who hear the call of holiness. It embodies in itself a way of life that discerns not the wisdom of this world but the foolishness of the Gospel. Long have contemplative monks and nuns been criticized for wasting their lives in an endless round of prayers and observances. Long have they endured the taunts, even the violence, of those who consider them barnacles on society and on the church. For they seem to do nothing with their lives except to pray and to give themselves over to the study of the science of the cross. Having been made fools for Christ by their entrance into the monastery and their strange way of life, they find, and only after long years and much suffering, and if God wills to give it, the way of perfect unity, first with Christ, then, in his transformation, in the movement of the Spirit through Christ back to the Father. From their cloister, they know the meaning of all things, the machinations of the human heart, and the foibles of the church. They know this because they have sat, sometimes for decades, with the shame of their own self-knowledge. Now, unashamed, they have sought the mercy of God and, by his grace, they have found it. Normally silent about such gifts, they nevertheless obey the popes who have asked that they share with the church their way of prayer.[4] This they have done magnificently

---

[4] Pope Paul VI, "A Select Anthology of Texts on Monasticism," trans. Francis Kline, *Cistercian Studies*, *Quarterly*, XX, 1985, n. 4, pp. 277–282.

through the ages, creating a storehouse for the church rich in narrated experience of the way to God. There is no better time than now to continue this sharing.

"Now when they saw the boldness of Peter and John and realized that they were uneducated and ordinary men, they were amazed and recognized them as companions of Jesus" (Acts 5:13). The Rule of St. Benedict includes a chapter which, in itself, is a summa of monastic teaching distilled from much earlier Christian monastic tradition. The seventh chapter on humility contains twelve steps of a ladder which ascends to God, even as we descend it by our actions of pride. By climbing these twelve steps the monk finds the answers to the hard questions posed by the parables of Jesus. He learns the wisdom of the cross, God's foolishness. He enters that stream of unity flowing from the cross as it makes its way back to God. The first several steps have to do with the fear of the Lord and continual prayer, the surrender of one's own way of doing things and the avoidance of the satisfaction of one's desires, and, obviously, obedience to superiors. The fourth step, the pivotal one in the scheme of twelve, asks the monk, in his obedience under difficult, unfavorable, or even unjust conditions, to embrace quietly the suffering at hand and to endure it without weakening or seeking escape (RSB 7:35). Once the monk has been able to round this all-important corner, he is ready for the more mature teaching of the ancients. Step five sees him readily seeking to divulge his secret sins and thoughts to the abbot, a sign of transparency and maturity in his spiritual life. From here, he begins a new phase of his journey into ordinariness and even nothingness.

The sixth step of humility teaches that a monk should be content "with the lowest and most menial treatment, and regards himself as a poor and worthless workman in whatever task he is given. . . ." (RSB 7:49). Gone are the ambitions of the brazen young. Absent, too, are the thoughts about the rights and privileges I think I deserve. This kind of humility is possible in an authentic way when a person has withdrawn from all posturing, from all the makeup of the persona one normally shows to the world. The very opposite of hubris and arrogance, it discerns in each situation the psychological field where people are jockeying for position as they relate to each other. The humble stance chooses not to object to inferior status quickly bestowed on those who refuse to fight for position. One cannot imagine the humble person grumbling against the landowner of the vineyard for paying him who has borne the heat of the day the same wage as the still-refreshed latecomer (see Mt. 20:1-16). Instead, he joins that great stream of humanity, but now with wisdom and knowledge that, in its daily duty to survive, thinks less about itself and more about others. A preoccupation of self gets swallowed up in commitments and duties that pass on life to others.

In the seventh step of humility, the monk "not only admits with his tongue but is also convinced in his heart that he is inferior to all and of less value, humbling himself and saying with the Prophet: "I am truly a worm, not a man, scorned by men and despised by the people (Ps. 21[22]:7)" (RSB 7:51-52). This harsh self-assessment follows directly in line with the christological interpretation of the Psalm just quoted. For we remember that Christ humbled himself, even to the point of death on the cross. He who, in the womb of the Holy Spirit, never left the Father in his divinity, accepted to be treated as one despised and rejected in his human form. In this sense is Christ willing to be of no account, becoming the very form of humility and meekness for our sake.

St. Paul, not divine but sharing in extraordinary gifts that put him on the level of the apostles so that he proclaimed himself an apostle, recognizes by means of his own self-knowledge as a persecutor of the church and a Pharisee of the Pharisees, that he is the least of the apostles and, in his own words, "unfit to be called an apostle because I persecuted the church of God. But by the grace of God I am what I am, and his grace toward me has not been in vain" (1 Cor 15:9b-10a). In the Letter to the Ephesians, St. Paul describes his humility in other terms: "Although I am the very least of all the saints, this grace was given to me to bring to the Gentiles the news of the boundless riches of Christ. . . ." (Eph. 3:8). St. Paul's humility, learned on the road to Damascus, was seared into his heart and never left him. It remained operative and normative in all the subsequent graces he received as the Spirit's mouthpiece for understanding in a particular and unique way Jesus of Nazareth. Humility in St. Paul was the matrix of his great power as an apostle and preacher, and as the forger of a new and divinely inspired christology, as well as his acceptance of martyrdom at the hands of the Romans. Step seven does not describe a wimpish, depressed person who willingly accepts the last place because he is afraid of venturing forth from it. Rather, the spiritual person refuses to be taken in by the attitudes of this temporal world, of seeking honors and prestige, of being thought well of, of maintaining a false, but polished, exterior that others are willing to allow. The spiritual strength of the humble one comes from the stark realization that everything one has, one has received. Always and everywhere, one remembers the evil lurking in the heart, the need for constant grace, and the gift of psychological balance to acknowledge freely one's inclinations to establish kingdoms, exercise power, and, in general, to take care of oneself at the expense of another. The humble person would never have objected to the king in the parable of the goats and sheep that he, gathered with the goats, had neglected the Lord. He would have readily admitted it, and he would have rejoiced at the selection of the others (the sheep) over him (see Mt. 25:31-46). He would have marveled at the gift of grace received by the blessed, and he would have gone onto his knees in sorrow and, no doubt, received the joy of repentance. But that response goes beyond the confines of the parable.

"The eighth step of humility is that a monk does only what is endorsed by the common rule of the monastery and the example set by his superiors" (RSB 7:55). Here we have the willing acceptance of confinement of one's ideas, one's preferences, and, above all, one's intelligence. The humble monk willingly lies hidden behind the observances of the house he lives in without questioning them, attempting to correct them, or finding fault with others who do not live up to them the way he thinks they should. He is following the example of his seniors (if there are any in his house). And he is humble enough, in the case of a silly rule or relaxed observance the community has foolishly agreed upon, to hide his criticism until he is asked for an opinion. In fact, he runs from any attempt to make him the founder of a clique or a group of dissidents in the monastery or to join one.

His choice for ordinariness and even disappearance within the community, especially if it be a large one, is fueled by his delight in the time and space it leaves him for prayer and the imitation of Christ, who had to correct his disciples to stop their arguing about who was the greater (see Mk. 9:33-37). The amount of energy that ordinariness saves a person, who no longer has to perform in a group in order to be validated, goes directly to the expansion of his wisdom and greater humility. Pregnant with the good things of discernment and consideration, he becomes a ripe fruit waiting to be plucked by the Holy Spirit and distributed for the enjoyment of the church.

"'Have you no answer? What is it that they testify against you?' But he was silent and did not answer" (Mk. 14:60b-61). The steps of humility continue with three grades that can be taken as one. Control of the tongue until one is asked a question (Step Nine), the avoidance of laughter that can degrade an encounter or hurt another (Step Ten), and the modesty and gravity of language (Step Eleven), all taken together form one of the glories of the monastic tradition, silence. Silence is a manifold thing. It begins as an exterior discipline which sets a tone for a monastic house and allows those who want to keep silent opportunities for an atmosphere conducive to prayer and recollection. This is an observance dictated by tradition and modulated in our day and age to an easier communication that fosters charitable communal living. People can keep silent for the wrong reason, and it is better to speak out what one cannot digest than to allow it to go sour in the heart. Nevertheless, the contemplative monk is preternaturally called to a silence that is always ready to listen to God, to allow the Spirit free reign to cleanse the monk's heart, which the Spirit will do even when confronted by the noise and puffed up speech of others. When the monk is ready, having climbed these many steps of humility, to rest at the borders of contemplation, he will, by his own desire, curb his tongue, lose his funny edge (without ever losing his sense of humor!), and graciously arrange his diction with gravity.

The summation and the goal for these various steps, the twelfth step, sees the monk living to the full one of Jesus' most eloquent parables. And this is no surprise, for the monks and nuns have always and only sought to keep the Scriptures and the teaching of the Gospels. We can focus ourselves on this passage or that, finding there a daily comfort and guide for our lives. But the monks and nuns make normative the parables that are hard to explain and that seem exaggerated. These they take to themselves as a way of trust in and insight into the Word of God. The parable we find at the twelfth step of humility is none other than the Pharisee and the Publican (Lk. 18:9-14). In the stance and attitude of the Publican, a tax collector for the Romans whom the Pharisees despised, we find the perfection of monastic humility. An outsider, considered a traitor to Israel, this man nevertheless exhibited a contrition that is what God waits for. The monks and nuns took the brief moment in the temple described in the parable and applied it to the whole of their lives. Conversion of heart, constant prayer, vigilance over the thoughts, all combine to produce this very Gospel-like attitude of near-constant compunction, based on a deep transformation of life.

> *The twelfth step of humility is that a monk always manifests humility in his bearing no less than in his heart, so that it is evident at the Work of God (the "Opus Dei," or choir offices), in the oratory, the monastery or the garden, on a journey or in the field, or anywhere else. Whether he sits, walks or stands, his head must be bowed and his eyes cast down. Judging himself always guilty on account of his sins, he should consider that he is already at the fearful judgment, and constantly say in his heart what the publican in the Gospel said with downcast eyes: "Lord, I am a sinner, not worthy to look up to heaven (Lk. 18:13)" (RSB 7:62-65).*

One must not take too literally this admirable description of a monk who has put on Christ. Another way to describe the attitude of the one constantly aware of the truth of our relationship to God is the knowledge of the passing of all things, the emptiness of the pride of life, and the degradation of the human body in the unbridled lust for pleasure. Over against this knowledge, the monks and nuns maintain their faith in the generosity of God who patiently waits for all of us to see the light of his presence, his Holy Spirit, in all of the things of the world, and to arrange our response to them accordingly.

Do not love the world or the things in the world. The love of the Father is not in those who love the world; for all that is in the world—the desire of the flesh, the desire of the eyes, the pride in riches—comes not from the Father but from the world. And the world and its desires are passing away, but those who do the will of God live forever (1 Jn. 2:15-17).

Monks and nuns see clearly the situation we are all in. They pray constantly for the world as it blunders along its violent and circuitous path. They are not depressed over it, since Christ has won the victory over sin and death in this world. All those who put on Christ to the extent portrayed in the twelfth step of humility enjoy a taste of this victory. They now experience what we all long for: an integration of our personhood, cleansed of the awful weight of duties, guilt, and compulsions.

Now, therefore, after ascending all these steps of humility, the monk will quickly arrive at that "perfect love of God which casts out fear" (1 Jn. 4:8). Through this love, all that he once performed with dread, he will now begin to observe without effort, as though naturally, from habit, no longer out of fear of hell, but out of love for Christ, good habit and delight in virtue. All this the Lord will by the Holy Spirit graciously manifest in his workman now cleansed of vices and sins (RSB 7:67-70).

By the work of the Holy Spirit, who joins him very closely to Christ, the monk is now ready for the more mature teachings of the Gospel as was outlined above. He can turn the other cheek to an assailant, do penance and rejoice over the election of the sheep, though he is a goat. He indulges in no grumbling when he is treated unfairly, since he harbors no resentment over those who get what perhaps they did not deserve. Finally, he is ready, when called to it, to give the shirt off his back when his neighbor is in need. He will go the extra mile and give without measure, just as it has been given to him.

. . . give, and it will be given to you. A good measure, pressed down, shaken together, running over, will be put into your lap; for the measure you give will be the measure you get back (Lk. 6:38).

Now that the monk is living the Gospel, he approaches that borderline between purification and love. For he has been tried in the fire of humiliation. He has learned by bitter experience of his sin that, love Christ as he will, there are other loves he chooses, even against his will, ahead of Christ. He cannot unite the loves, for Truth will not permit it. He is in despair until, according to God's grace, he knows the power of the Spirit to enter his life in an unexpected and, were it not so welcome and sought for, in an intrusive way, just as he prayed for it. His sin stops, his division is healed, his love for Christ is undivided, and from that love all other loves proceed in their proper order and place. The Rule describes this in Chapter 72, its penultimate chapter, on good zeal.

> *They (the brothers or sisters in community) should each try to be the first to show respect to the other (Rom. 12:10), supporting with the greatest patience one another's weaknesses of body and behavior, and earnestly competing in obedience to one another. No one is to pursue what he judges better for himself, but instead what he judges better for someone else* (RSB 72:4-7).

Is this passage not a perfect application of the scriptural description of authentic love, a love that is the mature fruit of the Baptism with the Holy Spirit and with fire in the living of the Gospel (Mt. 3:11)? Having arrived at that perfect love of neighbor that is possible only because one has loved God with the whole heart, the whole soul, and with all one's mind, and with all one's strength (Mk. 10:30), the monk stands at the threshold of the new creation. In him the ancient connection between God and the human person has been restored by the sacramental graces offered in Baptism and the Eucharist effectively received over time and through instruction and reflection. He has been called to the monastery by the Spirit of Christ to ask and search and knock with constant persistence at the door of the physical world to yield to him and reveal its truths planted there by the resurrection of Christ (see Lk. 11:9; 18:1-8). Through reformed attitudes, the constant purification of the thoughts, the quieting of the passions, and the discovery of a pure heart, the monk knows that he is now part of the new creation. The physical world, including his own body, becomes the place for enlightened behavior. The spiritual world includes the world we know in time and space. It is not that the physical has now obtained some measure of spiritual meaning, but, rather, that the physical is now diaphanous to the spiritual which has always encompassed it. The Spirit of God, sent out on mission by the Father to create the world according to the Word to be made flesh, that is, the Christ, allows those of belief to touch Christ, to believe in him, to be united with him, and to recognize the resurrected physical as spiritual, and the spiritual as glorified physical.

"The Lord's is the earth and all its fullness, the world and all its peoples" (Ps. 23[24]:1). The Rule ends with the startling admission that it is written only for beginners. If one lives it faithfully and to the full, then one is hastening to the heavenly homeland where one will need further instruction. This will be found on every page of the Scriptures, both the Old and the New Testaments, and in the writings of the ancients, the first writers in Christianity, and, of course, the monastic writers, especially, Basil, and the editors of the Lives of the Desert Fathers, and the Institutes and the Conferences of Cassian (we presume) (see RSB c. 73). All of this tradition brings the monk to the fullness of ecclesial living. For the monk is so joined to Christ that the Spirit of Christ now releases him from what St. Paul calls a fleshly relation with Christ to a spiritual one. The monk no longer needs to pray for himself and his needs. He has been cleansed to the point where he trusts completely in the Lord to save him. The monk now is swept up in that heavenly movement where Christ is seated at the right hand of the Father and interceding for all of us (see Heb. 7:23-25). The Spirit begins to bring the monk to that movement of increasing haste, urgency and vigilance in prayer, where he lives, no longer for himself, but is joined to that intercession to the Father which Christ makes for all those who approach him. Just as Christ, at the top of the ladder of humility, did not hesitate to breathe forth his Spirit to infuse further all those who follow Christ up the ladder, so that same Spirit infuses those who make haste, in their turn, to turn again and strengthen their brothers and sisters (see Lk. 22:31-32). The monk, having become one spirit with Christ (1 Cor 6:17), now also becomes with him a life-giving spirit (1 Cor 15:45). The monk stands with Christ who intercedes for us (see Rom. 8:34c). He joins that intercession because his union with Christ breathes into him the Spirit who intercedes for us with sighs too deep for words (see Rom. 8:26). Other mysteries unfold for the monk at this stage of contemplation. In turning back to help others who are also on the way, the monk learns the meaning of the parable of the sheep and the goats, that the whole world is challenged to identify Christ in all of the brothers and sisters, that everything is grist for the mystic mill of Christ, that the world only has meaning to the extent that it is taken up and fascinated with the idea of Christ, his goodness and his love. This is the unity he brings to the world. All else is vanity and perishes.

"Be alert at all times, praying that you may have the strength to escape all these things that will take place, and to stand before the Son of Man" (Lk. 21:36). The title "Son of Man" holds the key to the unity of which we speak. A divine title, with strong apocalyptic overtones, it tells of one sent from God who recapitulates in himself the entire creation and God's purpose for it. The divine person, called the Son of Man, however, appears from within the creation and not from outside it. This is the reason why all things are summed up in him. He is Son of the Father and, mysteriously, the unique cosmic person that stands for us all. In him, all of us stand before God in an ultimate destiny. It is also a human title, for it speaks of the begetting of Christ by Mary through the Holy Spirit in this world under the traditions of the Hebrew Law in which Christ took up our complete human experience. In his mystery, he chooses to be known as one of us who is also called to be one with him in his divinity. The way is through this world, as he is showing us constantly by his Spirit.

When Christ preaches in his church by his Spirit through the presider at Eucharist, he is saying that all the misfortunes we see in us and around us are the last times, the dreadful judgment, and the call to trust him and his election. He is saying that the dreadful injustice which grips so much of the world is already judged, and the works of injustice are already doomed to temporal destruction. He is saying that those who live without faith keep trying to make logical and human sense out of a world whose inner meaning escapes them because it lays claim to an eternal destiny. What Jesus describes as the distress of the last times has already been with us. In the hearts of the faithful, he is coming soon. In some, he has already arrived. The last times, proclaimed and preached during the Advent season with such ambiguity and reinterpretation by so many preachers in the church, is obviously the daily news of our journals.

> *There will be signs in the sun, the moon, and the stars, and on the earth distress among nations confused by the roaring of the sea and waves. People will faint from fear and foreboding of what is coming upon the world, for the powers of the heavens will be shaken . . . (Lk. 21:25).*

Christ is saying that all those who do not listen to his Gospel are doomed to a meaningless life of horrible thirst, dreadful groping, and paralyzing fear, all at the expense of others, in order to satisfy in this world something that can only be fulfilled through faith in him. Their judgment comes at the end of their lives and at the end of the world when there is no more hope of Gospel living. And the church must preach it.

> *Then they will see the Son of Man coming in a cloud with power and great glory. Now when these things begin to take place, stand up and raise your heads, because your redemption is drawing near* (Lk. 21:27-28).

But he is also saying that if one listens and follows and remains faithful, even though one may not see the results of good works, one is already standing before the Son of Man in the judgment, one is called and chosen, one is breaking through the barriers of time and space in service to others.

> *Be on guard so that your hearts are not weighed down with dissipation and drunkenness and the worries of this life, and that day does not catch you unexpectedly, like a trap. For it will come upon all who live on the face of the whole earth. Be alert at all times, praying that you may have the strength to escape all these things that will take place, and to stand before the Son of Man* (Lk. 21:34-36).

Living in such alertness gives the monks and nuns the wisdom to see how the world prepares itself for its destined meeting with Christ. This the ancient monastic writers called the First Natural Contemplation,[5] an insight into the order and goodness of all things since they are now seen through the eyes which the Spirit gives as the monks and nuns, and all those with them, make their way to the mystery of the One. For these the world is, indeed, at the end. It is also at the beginning of its glory.

The monks and nuns prepare the way for all those who bless the world in Christ's Spirit. They celebrate the liturgy, always seeking there the unity of Christ even in its manifold richness. They discover the compunction to which the readings in the liturgy call us. In their commitment and in their attitude of hospitality, they break down the barriers that maintain division in Christ's church, his people, and his children, wherever they may be. They do this by taking to themselves the hard sayings of the Gospels. In imitation of Christ, they become God's fools and find a way of wisdom that penetrates further into the narrow way of the Gospel. By their living the teaching of the ancients, they apply a theology to the experience of the written texts, especially that of the Rule of St. Benedict. They match what they read to what they experience of the economy of salvation, gaining knowledge of God, Father, Son and Holy Spirit through long centuries of reflection on his mystery. Their illuminative way of insight is unbroken in the church and, though deflated and inflated by declines and reforms, is kept healthy in its vigor and movement by the Spirit himself.

The monastic way is that ecstatic leap of the church to God. It is only a poor response to the leap of God to us through Christ in the Spirit. Though logically unnecessary in the church since the church celebrates the sacraments, the source and summit of the Christian life, it manifests the healing of the broken unity of the church. For the outlandish generosity of the monastic life comes from the outlandish generosity of God's love for us. In that ecstatic movement of God toward us and back to him is forged a new unity of all persons and things. The Spirit begins

[5] Evagrius Ponticus, *Kephalaia Gnostica*, ed. Antoine Guillaumont, *Patrologia orientalis*, XXVIII, fasc. 1, n. 134, Cinquieme Centurie, 51, n. 85, 87, 88; S2. n. 85. 87, 88, pp. 212–213; Sixieme Centurie, 51, n. 2, S2, n. 2, pp. 216–217.

to fold back into God all that is of Christ. Contemplative monks and nuns are grasped by the Spirit in this movement. The Spirit never lets go of them. The sacrifice of their lives is nothing compared to the joy of the movement of the Spirit back to God through Christ. In their ascension, they infuse the church with a joy that comes from the healing of divisions and the knowledge that the church is called and moving into the oneness Christ prayed for. Monks and nuns disappear in the church so that the Spirit's unity they have found in the sacraments and in the obedience of the Scriptures may pass to the whole church. Yet the monks and nuns remain in the Spirit with Christ as he makes his prayer, once uttered, but which continues forever:

> *I ask not only on behalf of these (his disciples), but also on behalf of those who will believe in me through their word, that they all may be one. As you, Father, are in me and I am in you, may they also be in us, so that the world may believe that you have sent me. The glory that you have given me I have given them, so that they may be one as we are one, I in them and you in me, that they may become completely one, so that the world may know that you have sent me and have loved them even as you have loved me (Jn. 17:20-23).*

New York City
The Feast of the Baptism of the Lord 2006

AFTERWORD

Prayer First: The Legacy of Francis Kline in the Key of C

Francis Kline was to me a friend, a brother, a father. When he phoned in May 2002 with news that he had been diagnosed with chronic lymphocytic leukemia, my world changed. He seemed to take the news of his illness lightly. It sent shock waves through my system.

What I often think of most when I look back on his life is his generosity. In that he was much like my own father. Francis was likely the most generous person I have ever known. He would give and give and give and spend and spend and spend. Anything he had and everything he had he wanted to give away, even and especially his own life. And this he did in ways beyond counting, in a manner and with a grace beyond the telling of it.

His heart got wider and wider and wider. But it never seemed to break. Love is like that. The wider it gets, the more it gives itself away, the more it has to give. Again and again. And yet again.

There was an ease in our exchange, and a candor that is the mark of deep friendship. I was very direct with him in offering my opinions and my criticisms. When he was still well, one of the senior brothers of Mepkin said to me: "Francis listens to Timothy of Gethsemani, to Peter of Guadalupe, and to you. If one of you can't get the point through to him, no one can." But this candor worked both ways, and it had its price. Francis would sometimes be quite hard on me, especially when he was very ill. When I apologized for things I had done that had apparently offended him, even before I could finish he said: "Don't give it another thought. We're brothers. We're friends. That's enough."

The last time I was with him was on the morning of July 12, 2006, after morning Mass. He asked to see me in the chapter room. We sat quietly. He told me that our time together at Mepkin had been all too short. I told him that he had been for me a friend, a brother, and a father over many years and across the miles. He demurred and said a few words about all I had been and done for him. I then told him that I would return for the big event at Mepkin on Labor Day, just weeks away, and the blessing of the Slaves' Cemetery together with the unveiling of Jonathan Green's painting, "Seeking," given by the artist as a gift to Mepkin. Francis perked up: "Oh! So I'll see you again soon. It will be great to see you. I'll be so looking forward to that."

As I opened the door of the chapter room and he went back into choir, he turned and smiled, offering his final words to me: "Hope springs eternal."

I have written of hope. More than anyone else in this world, Francis Kline helped me when my own hope began to wane. When hope was gone, Francis stirred it up in me again. My testimony to his generosity is to cling with every breath of my life to the hope by which he lived and in which he died.

Before my return to Mepkin for those end-of-summer events, he was gone from us. Just days before his passing, he sent word to the abbots and abbesses of the United States and Canada. In his illness his typing was poor, and so the letter is loaded with spelling errors and ellipses. I have taken the liberty to edit his final letter, avoiding paraphrase. Addressing himself to his fellow superiors in the region, he wrote:

> I came home [from Memorial Sloan-Kettering Cancer Hospital in New York] to Mepkin for good on March 16, 2006 and this is where I will stay. No more treatments, no more doctors' establishments, no more protocols or predictions.
>
> I was leaving New York for good. I was leaving the hospital, the doctor, everything. I knew God had spoken. Here is the formula I learned: God speaks. God doesn't speak. God does speak. Now He had spoken in a definitive way. My place was now Mepkin.
>
> I now am with God. He is my only option. I face the cancer with very little medical consultation, although there is a hospice doctor waiting in the wings should there be some question, and there have been many. The cancer is very active. It is not acting as we thought

it would. I have no opportunistic infections. Still, it has other means to make itself known.

God has spoken. His Word has changed me into a contemplative which I never thought I would become. By that I mean I feel totally taken over by God. Quite literally I have no one else. Nor do I wish for any one else. I wish that you would pray with me for this Mepkin community. This is how we remain united, when we pray with and for each other. In this unity of prayer, let us determine to run together toward the heavenly homeland. It is closer to all of us than we think.

Francis Kline

Mepkin Abbey
The Solemnity of the Assumption of the Blessed Virgin Mary, 2006

Francis Kline, monk of Gethsemani and third Abbot of Mepkin, died in the presence of his brother Ron and four others, just as the monks were filing into the infirmary after Vespers on August 27, the memorial of Saint Monica on the eve of Saint Augustine, Doctor of the Church, the great Doctor of Charity. Francis was buried alongside his brothers in the cemetery at Mepkin Abbey on a steamy Wednesday, August 30, 2006.

Though I had first caught glimpses of him while I was on sabbatical at the Abbey of Gethsemani in early January 1990, our first real exchange took place on a Sunday morning, the 21st of that same month. Under signature milky-oyster-grey-Kentucky winter skies, he had asked me to come to the novice master's office for a brief chat. His papers and other paraphernalia were strewn from one end of that small cubicle to the other. He was notoriously untidy with his personal effects. In that interval between breakfast and Sunday Mass, we conversed about all manner of things, but mostly about the things that were on my mind. My father was gravely ill, and I was burdened by thoughts of his impending death. In six long months he would be gone from us. In six minutes' time the life of the novice master I was just coming to know would be changed forever.

"So what's this I hear about you going to be elected abbot of some small, obscure monastery, one of Gethsemani's daughter-houses down south? Is it in North Carolina?" "South Carolina," he quipped, "the little state that God forgot!" and chuckled. "How do you say it? Is it Mempkin? Menkin?" He was gentle in his correction: "They say 'Mepkin.' It's a Native American word that means 'serene' or 'lovely.' It's beautiful; I've been there once. And there is no chance of my going there as superior, abbot, or anything else. Abbot Timothy has assured me that they have other plans. I'm off the hook. Let's talk about something else." And so we did. The phone rang moments later. "Sorry," he said as he crossed the room to pick up the phone. To the voice on the other end of the line: "Yes, Father?" I sensed it was Timothy. A long pause, perhaps for three full minutes. Then Francis to Timothy: "What do you want me to do?" Long pause. "I'll call you back before Vespers."

Hanging up the phone, he returned to the chair across from me. Silent. Ashen. "It happened, didn't it?" "Yeah," barely audible. "What do you want to do now?" I probed, aware that he might want to pass on the news to others, or ask to be alone for a minute. "Let's keep talking," he said, "say more about your father."

In part because we were together when the news of his election came, there grew deep bonds between us, the brothers, and the place called Mepkin. That initial conversation continued over the years and across the miles, ending just weeks before he died. From his abbatial election on January 21, 1990, through his long illness, excruciating diminishment, and death on August 27, 2006, our exchange was ongoing, albeit more spotty and somewhat strained in the last years of his life. Others in the Order of Cistercians of the Strict Observance may have come to know him better than I. No doubt he had his confidants. But he entrusted to me the task of telling what I knew of him and his life as an afterword to this book which we both knew in our marrow would be published posthumously.

How to tell the lines of a life loved and lamented by so many? More: How to convey to others the enduring legacy of a remarkable spiritual leader; a humble yet highly distinguished man of the church? What were his governing concerns, his core convictions, the passions that urged him on? That is my purpose here.

Born on December 21, 1948, the centenary of the foundation of the Abbey of Gethsemani in Kentucky, he was the first of three sons of Vanetta Hiltner and Joseph Paul Kline II. Joseph Paul

Kline III grew up in a similar environment to my own: working-class Catholic Philadelphia. He grew up in Nativity BVM Parish in Port Richmond; I in Most Blessed Sacrament Parish in Southwest Philadelphia. We breathed the same air. It was city air. The geography was that of tightly knit neighborhoods of row houses, with the parish church and school the centerpieces of our lives. He once said rather matter-of-factly: "I owe everything to the archdiocesan school system in Philadelphia." In particular there was Sister Anita Gertrude, ssj, his piano teacher.

We breathed the same air, walked the same city streets, but we moved in different circles: Joe went to the Jesuits' Saint Joseph's Prep; I to a less distinguished archdiocesan high school. This was followed by the young Mr. Kline's near-legendary launch to New York's Julliard School, the Bach recitals that we can still hear on the radio today, and the decision to follow a different course by knocking at the door of Gethsemani.

There is often a tendency to romanticize Joseph's seemingly abrupt departure from what might have been a very promising —perhaps world-class—career as an organist. Whatever mix of motives may lie beneath any decision any of us makes, I believe it is fair enough to say that Joseph entered Gethsemani because he wanted to give himself to God completely. Evidence of this is found in the letter he wrote to Timothy Kelly, then Abbot of Gethsemani, on October 17, 1974. In his formal request to make his first profession he writes:

> . . . the Church is asking me to follow the call of the Lord by making first profession. I wish to do so joyfully and with all my heart . . . I want this profession to be the beginning of a lifetime of giving to Him who, I strongly feel, wants to give me everything.
>
> I look upon the monastic life as the way to achieve the "fullness of life" even, in a gradual way, during the present life. Here, I can find the meaning of existence which is Christ.
>
> I can take him wholly to myself, I can serve him physically, concretely, and give him joy in my brethren.
>
> . . . I am sure my call is here at Gethsemani, where God seems to have prepared a place for me, among those who will take me as I am, where I can be myself before God and man.
>
> By living the Christian life here, I will come to know the joys and sorrows of all men. I will learn to live, not for myself, but for those

around me, for Christ. I will come to know more fully the poverty of life and its death, and the life of Christ and His Resurrection—a daily dying and rising, the mystery of Christian martyrdom.

It is in light of Francis's complete self-gift that his governing concerns, his passions, his convictions, and his loves are best understood. Here I shall line them up. Or play them out. I shall do so in the key of C. I am not a musician, but I know that the key of C is most basic, foundational, easiest; it is the key without accidentals, no sharps or flats; it is unembellished, unencumbered, plain, and unadorned; it is clean and clear, a delight to the ear. Even as I do so it is important to note that Francis himself never played in the key of C. It was too easy, too simple, too uncreative to do so. His life was, in my view, much too complex, layered, and intricate to be played out in C. But my purpose is to set down a record of how he might be remembered by those who may not have known him well, or not at all. And to do so simply.

Francis Kline was first and finally a man of the *church*. He loved the church from the time of his childhood until he breathed his last. His was that particular kind of Philadelphia Catholicism, with a strong focus on the diocese and on all its doings. He was immersed in the life of the local church. In most Philadelphia parishes in the 1950s, there was a strong sense of ethnic identity and local custom. Even as he glimpsed wider horizons, he had a strong sense of being part of a local community of believers. Whether in Port Richmond, Manhattan, Gethsemani, Rome, Mepkin, or Charleston, South Carolina, he was part of that local church. While every inch and ounce a monk, he was always alert to the goings-on in the diocese. Shortly after his blessing as Abbot of Mepkin, Francis became involved in the diocesan synod of Charleston and served as director of the diocesan office of worship. What some came to refer to as his fresh vision of monastic life for the future had everything to do with the fact that he saw the monastery as deeply and inextricably related to the life of the local church. Monks may have left the world on entering the monastery. But for Francis Kline, they were always part of the life of the church—the church universal to be sure. But it is in the local church where they live and work and pray, where they are bathed in the ebb and flow of liturgy and sacrament, that they live out their commitment to God.

Francis became friend and confidant to bishops, priests, and consecrated religious throughout the country, indeed throughout the world. He was in constant demand as retreat master, preacher, speaker, adviser. He struggled to balance these many demands with the requirements of his monastic rhythm. While he traveled in such circles, he never forgot his roots in Port Richmond, the geography of row houses and very ordinary—sometimes all too ordinary—people. He was strongly persuaded that God is best glorified when the greatest number of the baptized—ordinary laypeople—participate in the life of the church according to the measure of the gift given to each. He was unstinting in his support for the full flowering of the lay presence in the church. While he could be sharp in his critique of clerical and ecclesiastical, to say nothing of monastic, shortcomings, his love for the church—the whole church—was unwavering. For Francis, the monastic life was nothing more or less than immersion in the life flow of the church, which is to say immersion in the life of Christ, whose Body includes every member of the baptized.

Anyone who met him found in Francis Kline a man of *culture*. He loved art and architecture, literature and language, horticulture and harmony. He knew good wines from mediocre ones. His palate was delicate, though he would eat without complaint whatever was put before him. His years of study in Rome marked him forever, as did all those other places, France above all the rest. His insatiably curious mind took in everything he laid his eyes on. He couldn't get enough beauty. He could never see enough, hear enough, have enough of what his heart longed for. And then there was music. There are some who say that he was in ecstasy, outside himself, in another world, making love with those keys for laud of the Most High.

All this is to say that Francis was a highly "cultured" man, all the more amazing and appealing given his roots in working-class Philadelphia. But he also loved the culture of simple peoples. He loved the Gullah ladies who weave sweetgrass baskets on the streets of Charleston, as well as the neighbors of Berkeley County knocking at Mepkin's door for something to eat. He loved those knobs around Gethsemani and the locals of Nelson County with their near-hillbilly drawl. When Mepkin accepted paternity (sponsorship) of the Trappistine Monastery of Nuestra Señora de la Esperanza in Esmeraldas in Ecuador, Francis sought to master their language and learn their ways so that he could appreciate more deeply this community of Spaniards, *mestizas*, *indígenas*, mulattas and black sisters. While seeking care at Memorial Sloan-Kettering Hospital in New York, he loved to drink in the cultures of Haitian nurses, Jewish doctors, Filipino orderlies. When a struggling community of African monks in Illah, Nigeria, sought sponsorship of a Trappist monastery, Francis was their greatest advocate, traveling to their place and inviting some of their brothers to live at Mepkin. He himself offered to go there to help them get started in the ways of Cistercian life. He was every bit a classicist by training and by temperament. But this opened him up and out to see the riches of many different cultural expressions as something not just to be tolerated, but to be embraced and celebrated as a share in the life of the good God.

More than Trappist, Francis was **Cistercian**. Though he did not much cotton to the works of Thomas Merton, like him Francis was more interested in the Cistercian patrimony than its Trappist trappings. He wanted to get back to the fathers and the founders, to their original orientations beneath layers of law and practice that could obfuscate the lightness of the burden Christ promised to those who follow him. For Francis it was a simple matter of following Christ, simple and poor, wherever he led. This means being soaked in Scripture—day in and day out—being bound to love a particular group of brothers at a specific time and place, here and now, doing whatever work was his to be done in service of their common life of prayer. And it was this that was always foremost. Prayer. He was unfailing in this, his first, commitment. Much is made of the transformation of the campus at Mepkin during the abbatial ministry of Francis Kline. But it needs always to be remembered that the first item on the agenda of the community under its new Abbot Francis was to build a new church, what the monks at Mepkin call "A House for the Church of Mepkin." Luminous, simple, a mix of Scandinavian-and-Shaker-barn in feel, the Church of Mepkin stands as a soaring reminder to the legacy of Francis Kline and the other poor brothers of Mepkin. Stark and spare, simple yet stunning, it is in every way a jewel that is Cistercian through and through. It is a compelling icon of the whole Cistercian way: Prayer first!

At Mepkin I would often sit with Abbot Francis mulling over some theological conundrum or concern in the church when the bell would call us to pray. After allowing me to finish my sentence —or the last sip of a good wine—he would rise from his chair and whisper: "Prayer first." And we would race off for Compline at day's end.

Francis seemed a bit uneasy with the term "contemplation" or contemplative prayer. Strangely, he did not think it fit him—his way of life or his way of prayer. He would quietly insist that monks pray much like any other believer might pray. But they do it in common and they do it seven times a day. Every day. All the time. But the distinctive characteristics of contemplation— quiet receptivity to God's initiative; wonder; attentiveness to God's presence in human life, history, the world, and the church; a sort of intuitive experiential feel for the ways of God; an enduring sense of being lured and led by God in all things—all these marked the life of Francis Kline. He could be busy, distracted, racing, late for meetings, sometimes impatient, and a bit chiding when he felt pressed or pushed into a corner. But there could be no doubt that he was *contemplative* to his core, or at least a contemplative-in-the-making: "Prayer first." And always.

One look at the land called Mepkin reveals the care it has been given from generation to generation. Francis saw this beautiful plantation as a gift, not just for the monks but for the people of South Carolina's Lowcountry. In the face of efforts to encroach on the land, to cut it up and parcel it out first for this purpose then for that, Francis Kline raised his voice in the public square in an effort to conserve the land, not just at Mepkin and for his brothers; he also became a champion for the conservation of the grassy lands and silken waterways of the wider Lowcountry. Critics of priests "meddling in politics" abound. Never was this criticism raised about Francis, first a monk, whose whole way of life is about conservation: of the ways of prayer; of ancient religious discipline; of gospel values; of earning a living from the land while making peace with its ways and its wonders; of a harmony that will not yield to our proclivity to plunder for our own purposes. That Francis was a *conservationist* of the land is just one facet of the many strains of a long tradition he sought to conserve.

If Francis was a conservationist, of the land and of a long tradition of core monastic ways and values, he also sought to *communicate* the monastic way and wisdom to the wider church and world. With his exquisite musical talent, his ability to captivate an audience with his spiritual teaching—never with a prepared text or even a slip of paper near at hand!—with his shimmeringly shy reverence for everything going on in the church and the world—and for everyone who crossed his path—people readily recognized him as a bearer of the Word and the Spirit. People of all sorts were drawn to him. With oversized glasses and little care for the way he dressed or put himself together, Francis often looked a bit disheveled. Clothes, haircuts, and glasses simply didn't matter to him. People of all sorts could see that he lived and loved something very deeply. And he communicated that One Love with his every step, with every glance he gave, with the air he took, and the breath he left behind.

It was, in the end, all about *Christ* as far as Francis was concerned. He had an almost enviable love of Christ. It was a love born of knowledge. He spoke of Christ as one who knew him, who loved him completely. In any spiritual conference, in any of my appeals to him in my little crises, he would always, unfailingly and often frustratingly, turn the whole thing on its heels so that I—we—were forced to look Christ in the face. I don't mind saying that I have never known anyone of whom I could say without equivocation: He loves Christ. Whatever may be said of Francis, in the end it must be said that, following the exhortation of his holy father Benedict, he preferred nothing to the love of Christ (Rule of Benedict 72).

In the end it was Francis who had to stand face-to-face with Christ, as we all must do. His diminishment and death were embraced with faith and without fanfare. On the feast of Saint Benedict, July 11, 2006, we sat together for the last time in his abbot's office. He narrated a few of the difficulties he had to endure during the nights of the previous several years: night sweats, sleeplessness, repeated changing of bedclothes. There were other details of the sort you wouldn't talk about in polite company. He said little about the loss of feeling in his feet and hands—those hands that once made love to God through the blacks and whites of an organ. I told him that I could not imagine how painful it must be. "It's not unpleasant," he said with a smile. "That's not to say it's easy." He added: "Michael, I'm on the edge. I get out of bed in the morning, I put my feet on the floor, and I say: 'I want to live.'" His chin quivered and he wept unsparingly. I stood up and embraced him so that the tears would find some human soil into which to fall. He looked up: "I love God. And I love what God is doing."

It was then time for one last ride. We had traveled so many times before—together to so many different places. He always insisted on driving the car. Always "in charge." Friends and brothers, yes. But he was the abbot. He wanted to drive around the grounds of Mepkin, a place he had come to know like the fingers of a blind old woman know the letters of her Bible in braille. He wanted to spot an alligator in the lake. But they were quiet and sleepy that July afternoon. We then drove by the chicken houses as "the girls" squawked and squealed in the blazing heat. Outside was parked a truck that the monastery had just acquired for egg deliveries—a used truck that once distributed "Little Debbie" cakes and cookies. He had an insatiable sweet tooth. "God, I wish that truck was full of Little Debbies—don't you just luv'em?—I could eat every damned one of them!" He looked over, wrinkled his nose, and laughed like an eight-year-old.

With minutes remaining before Vespers, he wanted to push on to the banks of the Cooper River at the edge of the property. He stopped the car and we sat. I waited for some small snippet of wisdom he wanted to leave me. None came. "I hear those wood frogs every night. I don't sleep. A concert of voices. I love them. Always the same. Beautiful. But always the same song. I'm tired, Michael." He turned toward the edge of the Cooper as if to command the wood frogs directly: "Sing me something different tonight, will you, you beautiful things?" When we parked the car near the monastery door, just in time for Vespers, I opened the door for him so he could get out of the driver's seat. He lifted his hand to me and asked quietly: "Can you help me please?" I knew then that his hour was near.

It is often enough said that Francis was childlike. The man I knew was far too complex, in some ways conflicted, to be called childlike. But, my God, could he play. He knew when to play, what to play, how to play. That he could play an organ as if making love to God is one of the legacies he has left us, part of a public record, if a monk has a public record. But what he also left was the legacy of one who—with wrinkled nose and a weeeeeeeeee eeeeeeeeeeeeeeeeeeeeeeeeee! of a laugh—was buoyed up and brimming over with the magnitude of God's love, God's goodness, God's delight.

Francis brought sheer delight to the lives of those he touched. He lived and frolicked in life true to the name he was given by Timothy: Francis. His was the delight that comes from knowing oneself to be a fool for Christ—like the Poor Man of Assisi for whom he was named; or a plaything in the hands of his Lover, like Thérèse of Lisieux, whose small black-and-white photo was at Francis's bedside when he breathed his last. Even at the end he could chuckle: "It's not unpleasant. I love what God is doing."

From the streets of Port Richmond and Nativity, BVM, to Saint Joe's Prep and Julliard, from Gethsemani and Rome, and finally to the infirmary at Mepkin Abbey, his heart marveled with delight at what God was doing in him, in all of us, and in God's wonder-filled world.

"Prefer nothing to the love of Christ." For Francis this was not a chore. It was a yoke easy, a burden light—even while he bore the weight of so much and so many. Even as he carried the heavy cross of his suffering—and fulfilled his duties as abbot until the end—he knew that it was he who was being carried in life and in death to the breast of his beloved Christ where he now rests.

Michael Downey
Covenant Brother, Mepkin Abbey
Cardinal's Theologian, Archdiocese of Los Angeles
Professor of Systematic Theology and Spirituality,
Saint John's Seminary

Joseph Paul Kline III
Dom Francis, Third Abbot of Mepkin

Born: December 21, 1948, Philadelphia, Pennsylvania

Graduate: Saint Joseph's Preparatory School, Philadelphia, 1966
Graduate: Julliard School of Music, B.S., Organ, June 4, 1971
Graduate: Collegio San Anselmo, Rome, STB, magna cum laude,
    September 18, 1984

Entered Gethsemani: June 12, 1972
Solemn Profession: December 8, 1977
Ordained Priest: January 12, 1986

Elected Third Abbot of Mepkin: January 21, 1990
Abbatial Blessing: March 19, 1990

Died: August 27, 2006